En

MW01291277

"I believe we all long to know the deeper things of God. *Deeper Still* is a must read if you want hope and faith to be built in your heart to know the secrets to a life of deeper trust and understanding of how prayer touches the heart of God. Debbie Przybylski has a heart for God and she writes with a profound understanding of the ways of God. She has been tested with fire and writes with that deeper kind of faith that is produced in the furnace of affliction."

FLOYD McCLUNG
President of All Nations, South Africa
Former International Executive Director
Youth with a Mission (YWAM)
Best-selling author

"Don't let the title fool you. This is not another book to help you simply learn more about prayer; it is a primer for how to apply prayer in many of the neglected areas of spiritual discipleship. *Deeper Still* is a Biblical and practical call to action for every Christian and any congregation, a resource for prayer leaders to use with their prayer teams and prayer ministries. Scan the Table of Contents and you'll discover that by going deeper, you will take your people upward and forward!"

PHIL MIGLIORATTI
Founder, National Pastors' Prayer Network
Coordinator of Loving Our Communities to Christ

"Debbie had laid out a powerful guideline in the power and anointing we are called to in prayer. She takes us deeper in the Holy Spirit and the intimate and strategic places of the Lord, encouraging us to pursue God's love, to walk in the His presence, submitting our lives in a personal relationship to Him. We have a rich inheritance in the Kingdom of God, called to partner with the Lord in hearing His heart and voice and agreeing with Him in prayer. *Deeper Still* will challenge and take you on a journey into the cherished and hidden places of the Lord and release you to be an anointed, empowered, effective intercessor and warrior. Thank you, Debbie for writing this book."

BECCA GREENWOOD
President
Christian Harvest International
Author

"Deeper Still: Secrets to a Deeper Prayer Life by Debbie Przybylski is a Holy Spirit packed guidebook heralding the power of prayer for today. By masterfully placing within reach God honoring insights on how to prepare for prayer for ministers, missionaries and the like-minded who love the Lord, Debbie dares us to examine more fully what God has empowered us to do. We really can more effectively exercise divine reach in this world through prayer. I love this book."

OLIVIA M. MCDONALD
Professor, Regent University
Director of National Day of Prayer
Virginia Beach, VA

"Debbie's writing ministers to my heart on a deeply spiritual level. Behind Debbie's words is a heart that longs after an intensely personal love relationship with God. I take my time to read what she writes with a listening ear to catch what God's Spirit wants to teach me. I also value Debbie's open and honest sharing of some very personal issues and how God has used such experiences to train her to pray with hope in the face of uncertainty and even anxiety. Finally, I find myself impacted by Debbie's prophetic message, confronting me with the urgency to intercede for the nations while God still gives them the opportunity to respond to His love by putting their trust and hope in His Son, Jesus."

GRAHAM ROBERTS
Equip & Encourage International
Sydney, Australia

Deeper Still

Secrets to a Deeper Prayer Life

The Intercessors Arise Books

Debbie Przybylski

Foreword by Gwen Shaw
Founder and President: End-Time Handmaidens, Inc.

Deeper Still
Secrets to a Deeper Prayer Life

Debbie Przybylski
www.intercessorsarise.org

CreateSpace: Charleston, SC

ISBN-13: 978-1449988128
ISBN-10: 1449988121

Dedication

∻

This book is dedicated
to all who want to go deeper
with God in prayer.
May the Lord
bless you richly
with treasures in the deep
as you seek to know Him better.
May you go deeper in prayer
and intimacy with God
than you ever
dreamed possible.

Contents

❧❧

Discover the holiness of God and the attitudes we need to develop in light of His awesome holiness. Learn Biblical truth about the providential care of God and how this relates to your prayer life. Discover how to respond to God's holiness and providential care in your own personal prayer life. Awaken your heart to a deeper relationship with God.

If we want a deeper prayer life, we must understand the supremacy of Christ. Discover how the Scriptures, historical accounts, and humanity present His supremacy. Jesus was the greatest intercessor on earth. Find out about His position as intercessor in heaven, and discover how to partner with Him on earth. Learn how to celebrate His supremacy; grow deeper in glorifying Him in your worship and prayer life.

The Holy Spirit's Ministry and Power
The Holy Spirit and Praying for the Lost
Deeper Still Life Application

There are many descriptions of the Holy Spirit in Scripture. Discover the vast ministry of the Holy Spirit, and learn about this supernatural prayer partner. Find out how the Holy Spirit is working powerfully in the world, and learn ways to join Him in praying for the lost. A prayer of repentance is included in this chapter.

Chapter Four
Deeper in Strategic Prayer   69

Prayer is the Strategy of Heaven
Prioritizing Prayer
Strategic Joy in the Midst of Warfare
Deeper Still Life Application

Prayer gives us heaven's strategy to do the work on earth that will change the world. In this chapter learn how to grow deeper in strategic prayer. Receive understanding through the Biblical, historical, and personal examples of earnest prayer warriors who prioritized prayer. Discover the cost, and learn how living strategically is a key to victory. Find out how to find joy in prayer in the midst of warfare.

Chapter Five
Deeper in Spiritual Insight   89

Praying with Insight
Enthroning God through Prayer Mapping
Crafted Prayer
Deeper Still Life Application

When we pray God gives us insight into life situations. Discover ways you are empowered when you seek God for insight, wisdom, and discernment. Find out how to pray that will enhance spiritual insight. Learn how to enthrone God in your neighborhood, your city, and your nation through prayer mapping. Become aware of Biblical examples where this was done effectively. Discover how to write a crafted prayer; learn to pray specific, on-target prayers for yourself, your family, and your church.

Chapter Six
Deeper in Disciplining the Soul   105

The dark night of the soul is common to all who are seeking God wholehearted. Learn the secret of brokenness and how to grow deeper in disciplining the soul. Discover the purpose and benefits of God's stripping process and how to face the dark night of the soul successfully. Learn Biblical prayers of lament, and study the example of Habakkuk 3:17-18. Find guidelines on how to write your own prayer of lament, and learn how to benefit from seasons of hiddenness.

Chapter Seven
Deeper in Effective Prayer   123

Find out what happens in the impossible place when you pray. Discover how the power of God is released when you face the impossible and pray in fervent faith. Learn the importance of perseverance in prayer. Consider possible hindrances that can block your prayer life. Discover ways to increase your perseverance and grow deeper in effective prayer.

Chapter Eight
Deeper in a Lifestyle of Fasting   139

We all need to be encouraged to grow deeper in a lifestyle of fasting and prayer. Learn about the purifying power of fasting and prayer, and become aware of the various fasts in Scripture. Find out how fasting and prayer can break through burdens, setting the captives free. Learn how to fast the right way with the right heart, and consider the benefits of fasting found in Isaiah 58:5-12. Grow deeper in a lifestyle of fasting by receiving practical steps for your own life.

Passion and fervency in prayer is a key to victory. In this chapter you will learn about the power of crying out. Discover how to pray passionate prayers that bring transformation to your family, city, and nation. Learn how to have passion for revival, and find out why desperation is the key to transformation.

The purpose of our life is to pursue God. This chapter will awaken you to what the Bible says about pursuing God's presence. Discover Scriptural roadblocks to God's presence and barriers that prevent God's entrance into our cities and churches. Become aware of what God's manifest presence looks like and how things change when the glory of God enters a city. Learn how to cultivate God's presence in your city and how to personally go deeper in God's presence in your pray life.

Foreword

It is through the fires of testing that we are taken deeper into God's presence and deeper into a life of prayer. Our hour of desperation can be our finest hour if we turn to God, who is the only One who can meet us at that point. Debbie met God in her hour of desperation and together with the Holy Spirit has given us the fruit of that meeting combined with years of training by Him in prayer. This book, *Deeper Still: Secrets to a Deeper Prayer Life*, is one of those anointed books that captivates the heart and draws one closer to God. Debbie challenges the reader not only to a life of prayer but of communion with God in a place of hiddenness, a place that she herself has found and can write about with clarity.

You, the Reader, are embarking on a wonderful journey. As you open this book, you will find answers to your many questions and you WILL find the secrets to a deeper prayer life within these beautifully written pages, secrets that have been well worked out in the author's life. Thank you Debbie, for pressing in to God and giving us this beautiful gift from Him.

DR. GWEN R. SHAW
Founder and President
End-Time Handmaidens, Inc.

Acknowledgments

With special thanks:

To the Holy Spirit, for Your help and partnership in writing this book. You gave me perseverance and encouragement every day, and I am extremely grateful. I learned so much about your heart for intercession, and I am so blessed in being part of this worldwide prayer movement.

To my husband Norman, who persevered with me in every one of these books about prayer. Thank you for releasing me to be an intercessor and writer.

To Jeanne Allen, Debbie Leseberg, and Robin Saboda, who gave many hours of hard work in editing this book on prayer. Thank you so much for all your help.

To the Elijah Company, Inc., Board of Directors, who have helped us in the ministry of Elijah Company, Inc. and Intercessors Arise International. Thank you for your encouragement and prayers. We appreciate you so much.

To our friends and extended family, who encouraged us along this journey of writing about prayer and world missions. You are so important to us. Thank you for being such a blessing in our lives.

To the intercessors, who have prayed for us throughout the years. We are so thankful for your prayers.

Introduction

Deep calls to deep in the roar of your waterfalls;
all your waves and breakers have swept over me.
By day the LORD directs his love, at night his song is with me—
a prayer to the God of my life.
Psalm 42:7-8

This book, *Deeper Still: Secrets to a Deeper Prayer Life*, is very special to me because I wrote most of it during the time I was facing breast cancer. It was in *Deeper Still* while recovering from cancer that most of these teachings on prayer were formulated and designed.

This book focuses on the deep, inner life of those who are seeking God in prayer. I had been an intercessor for over 35 years and felt I had learned many spiritual lessons in prayer, but I discovered that God wanted me to go *deeper still*. When the waves and storms of life were sweeping over me, I found God as my song in the night and as the prayer of my life.

The first three chapters of *Deeper Still* will bring you into a deeper understanding of the Trinity—the Father, Son, and Holy Spirit. With the understanding of the Trinity as the foundation, it moves into various secrets to a deeper prayer life. You will learn how to go deeper in strategic prayer, spiritual insight, and persevering prayer. You will become aware of the secrets of a hidden lifestyle and how to discipline your soul in prayer. You will discover how to fast successfully, pray with insight, and develop crafted prayers. You will also learn how to become passionate in pursuing God's presence in your own life, in your city, and your nation. With thirty separate teachings on prayer, you will learn a wide array of secrets to help you go deeper with God.

Go through this book slowly, and drink deeply from each chapter. Each one has three separate teachings that take in a different aspect of the theme of that chapter. I have spent many hours in the presence of the Lord as I thought, prayed, and wrote about each topic. They are short and highly motivational. *Deeper Still* is designed in such a way that you can easily use it to teach others about the secrets to a deeper prayer life. The life application at the end of each chapter makes it easy to make it real in the lives of others as well as your own life. The chapters end with "My Prayer to God." These are crafted prayers that you can pray again and again.

May God richly bless you as you launch forth in this exciting adventure of intimacy with God. May He give you songs in the night and deep treasures all along the journey as He brings you *deeper still* in your personal prayer life. My prayer for you is that He will take you further and deeper in prayer than you ever imagined possible. I pray that *Deeper Still: Secrets to a Deeper Prayer Life* prepares you for your destiny and journey with God in this changing world in which we live.

May you begin with great faith and anticipation in what God will do in your prayer life. God is calling you *deeper still*. Enjoy the journey.

CHAPTER ONE

DEEPER IN KNOWING GOD

I keep asking that the God of our Lord Jesus Christ,
the glorious Father, may give you the Spirit
of wisdom and revelation,
so that you may know him better.
Ephesians 1:17

WHEN THE GLORY OF GOD filled the house of the Lord, the priests could not perform their service because of the cloud (1 Kings 8:11). Imagine if the glory of God came sweeping into your church and touched you and every church member so deeply that you couldn't even stand. In Revelation 15:8a we read about the glory of God filling the temple with smoke so dramatically that no one could even enter.

> *And the temple was filled with smoke from the glory of God and*
> *from his power, and no one could enter the temple...*

God's glory was much too powerful!

There is a story about an Emperor called Trajan who once asked a Christian, "Why can't God be seen by mortal eyes? If God is everywhere as you Christians say, I want to see Him." The Christian said, "Yes, God is everywhere but no mortal eye can behold His glory."

But the Emperor wanted a better explanation. This one wasn't good enough. The Christian thoughtfully said to him, "Let's go and look at one of His ambassadors." They walked outside together, and he pointed to the dazzling sun in the sky. It was so bright that the Emperor could not look straight at the sun, but had to squint with his eyes nearly shut as he looked up into the bright, blue sky. The Christian replied, "Can you look at one of His creatures? If you can't, how can you hope to look upon the Creator Himself and live?"[1]

As you begin this book, I pray that God will open your heart to a deeper revelation of Himself in His dazzling beauty with a much deeper understanding of the many dimensions of prayer and intercession. I pray that each chapter will be a personal stepping stone in your walk with God into a deeper and more fulfilling prayer life. Just as the Emperor Trajan could not see God with His mortal eyes, we can never see or exhaust the many facets of prayer and intercession. It is too deep a subject to adequately behold, but God can bring us further in our experience of prayer than we've ever been before.

You may be wondering, "How can I know God in a deeper way? Is there a way that I can grow deeper in my effectiveness in prayer? How can I have a successful prayer life?' As you begin realize that God wants to teach you about Himself. He wants to teach you about strategy and insight in prayer. He desires to make you more effective in intercession. In this first chapter, we will look at the holiness of God and our response to that revelation. Learn about the providential care of God and how this relates to your personal prayer life.

The Holiness of God

Day and night they never stop saying: "Holy, holy, holy is the Lord God Almighty, who was and is, and is to come." Whenever the living creatures give glory, honor and thanks to him who sits on the throne and who lives for ever and ever, the twenty-four elders fall down before him who sits on the throne, and worship him who lives for ever and ever. They lay their crowns before the throne and say: "You are worthy, our Lord and God, to receive glory and honor and power, for you created all things, and by your will they were created and have their being (Revelation 4:8b-11).

The holiness of God is an absolutely awesome topic; what an appropriate way to begin this book on prayer. The four living creatures and the twenty-four elders in the throne room of heaven were able to see God in His holiness, and when they did they fell down to worship Him, laying their crowns at His feet.

We need to see God in His holiness. Think about it. A glimpse of a holy God should cause us immediately to bow to our knees and cry out as the prophet Isaiah did in Isaiah 6:5: *"Woe is me!" I cried. "I am ruined! For I am a man of unclean lips, and I live among a people of unclean lips, and my eyes have seen the King, the LORD Almighty."* As I have personally entered into more day and night prayer over the past few years, I am brought to the point where I say:

"O God, You are so great, so holy, and I am so undone and in need of You. Help me. Cleanse me, and bring me into Your holiness."

If we want to go deeper in knowing God, it is so important to seek to know His holiness in our personal life. God wants us to set ourselves apart for His purposes and not mix with the evil in the world. Purity and holiness are essential for standing in His holy place and receiving blessings from Him. God answers the prayers of those who have clean hands and a pure heart, those who have learned to walk in holiness. We read in Psalm 24:3-6:

> *Who may ascend the hill of the LORD? Who may stand in his holy place? He who has clean hands and a pure heart, who does not lift up his soul to an idol or swear by what is false. He will receive blessing from the LORD and vindication from God his Savior.*

Years ago we rarely used dryers for our clothes, and most women would hang their newly washed clothes outside on the clothesline to dry. I remember how these clean, fresh clothes would blow gently in the breeze. One woman was so proud of how white her clean clothes looked, she thought they were absolutely shining. But it snowed that afternoon, and her yard was blanketed in white. When she looked at them and observed the snow next to her clothes, she exclaimed, "Look at God's almighty snow against my plain white clothes! There is no comparison."

There is a radiance of God's holiness, and nothing on earth can begin to compare with Him. He is so holy and so pure in all of His splendor and beauty. We may think we are clean and righteous, but next to

God's holy and pure radiance we realize that we are undone and need His cleansing.

God wants to be known by His holiness.

It is the attribute that He uses to describe Himself. It is also the crowning attribute in which all the other attributes are contained—His love, purity, goodness, kindness, and beauty. If we want to know God, we have to know His holiness. In our evangelism efforts we often tell about the works of God, but not about God Himself. Jesus calls us to testify about Himself.

We must realize that the people around us lack knowledge of a holy God. We are the ones who can point them to His holiness. We are the ones who can reflect God's holiness in our own personal lives. If we want to be fruitful and effective in our prayers, we need to seek to know God's holiness. In Isaiah 6:1-7, let's look at two acts that reveal God's holiness; the appearance and provision for holiness.

The Appearance of Holiness

In the year that King Uzziah died, I saw the Lord seated on a throne, high and exalted, and the train of his robe filled the temple. Above him were seraphs, each with six wings: With two wings they covered their faces, with two they covered their feet, and with two they were flying. And they were calling to one another: "Holy, holy, holy is the LORD Almighty; the whole earth is full of his glory." At the sound of their voices the doorposts and thresholds shook and the temple was filled with smoke (Isaiah 6:1-4).

Have you ever thought about what a holy God looks like?

Holiness is the signature of the divine. It is the attribute by which all others are related. Even the sum of all the attributes of a holy God is insufficient to exhaust its meaning. God is perfect and flawless.

If you have experienced the presence of God in His holiness, there is always something more that resists formulation or definition. Wherever God's presence is felt, there men encounter the wonder and mystery of holiness.

- **God's holiness does not fit human description.** It is not rational; it is super-rational (above the limits of the mind). We have no language to describe it.

- **God's holiness can be experienced.** There are many ways you can learn and experience God's holiness. You can know holiness through the written Word of God, through creation, fellowship with others, worship, prayer, and personal discipleship.

- **God's holiness is viewed through Isaiah 6:1-4.** This shows us His power, greatness, and loftiness. Glory and majesty exhibit His uniqueness and separateness, His being set apart. He is incomparable. *"To whom will you compare me? Or who is my equal?" says the Holy One* (Isaiah 40:25).

Who among the gods is like you, O LORD? Who is like you— majestic in holiness, awesome in glory, working wonders? (Exodus 15:11)

The Provision for Holiness

Then said I, Woe is me! For I am undone and ruined, because I am a man of unclean lips, and I dwell in the midst of a people of unclean lips; for my eyes have seen the King, the Lord of hosts! Then flew one of the seraphim [heavenly beings] to me, having a live coal in his hand which he had taken with tongs from off the altar; And with it he touched my mouth and said, Behold, this has touched your lips; your iniquity and guilt are taken away, and your sin is completely atoned for and forgiven (Isaiah 6:5-7, Amplified).

Is there provision in light of our unworthiness and unholiness?

As we see how holy God is and sense our own undoneness, there is a provision for us! It is Christ's righteousness. Our sin is atoned for through the death of Jesus Christ. Jesus takes away our guilt and gives us a new way to live—it is the way of holiness. He shows us his Fatherly discipline. It doesn't always feel good and might be quite painful, but through His discipline we can share in His holiness. We can become more like Him.

- **Christ's righteousness.** Christ's righteousness is our provision for holiness. God's holiness constitutes a need for atonement. Jesus became sin for us so that we might become the righteousness of God (2 Corinthians 5:21).

  In bringing many sons and daughters to glory, it was fitting that God, through whom everything exists, should make the pioneer of their salvation perfect through what he suffered (Hebrews 2:10).

- **Fatherly discipline.** God requires holiness because He provided it in Christ. Because God is holy, He will discipline us unto holiness. Without holiness our message will lack credibility. When God's people fail to show His holiness, then God displays His holiness through discipline.

  They disciplined us for a little while as they thought best; but God disciplines us for our good, in order that we may share in his holiness. No discipline seems pleasant at the time, but painful. Later on, however, it produces a harvest of righteousness and peace for those who have been trained by it (Hebrews 12:10-11).

Put on some beautiful worship music, take your shoes off in holy reverence, and kneel before your Almighty God. Let Him touch you until you are undone in His presence—let Him wash you clean and remold you—let Him break through into your heart where you feel His heart and sense His incomparably great holiness. Let His throne room captivate you, and no earthly king or president will overly impress you. Just as the woman's white wash was dull in comparison with God's beautiful snow, nothing on this earth compares with the beauty and holiness of God.

Do not resist any discipline God may be bringing into your life, because it is through this discipline that you can share in His holiness. It is through His discipline that a harvest of righteousness is produced. Say, "Yes" to all His personal ways with you. Let Him take you deeper than you've ever been before. Let Him change your heart today through the splendor and majesty of His holiness.

An exalted view of God brings a clear view of sin and a realistic view of self. A diminished view of God brings a reduced concern for sin and an inflated view of self. Isaiah may have been satisfied with his personal holiness until he saw the Lord in His unspeakable glory. Isaiah's encounter with holy God made him immediately and keenly aware of his own unholiness and the sinfulness of those around him. It is impossible to worship God and remain unchanged. The best indication that we have truly worshiped is a changed heart.[2] Henry and Richard Blackaby, *Experiencing God Day-by-Day*

Our Response to God's Holiness

When King Uzziah died, then the prophet Isaiah began to see God as He really is. And when he began to see God, he also began to see himself to—as he really was! "... I am a man of unclean lips." When God opens our eyes, He opens them so we can see in both directions. We can see God as He is, and we can also see ourselves as we are. One-directional vision is not enough. In fact, we cannot see ourselves as we really are, in need of the Savior, until we see God as He is, in His uncompromising holiness.[3] Eugenia Price, *Share My Pleasant Stones*

As we look at the awesome holiness of God, what should our response be? How should we prepare ourselves to meet with a holy God?

We must realize that there is a way of holiness that is always a narrow path, a special highway that few walk on. God wants us to walk on this highway of holiness, motivating others to earnestly seek Him as they watch our lives. He wants to remove every obstacle in our life that hinders His divine outflow so that His holiness might shine through. As we see God in His uncompromising holiness, we see ourselves more clearly and the sin areas in our lives. This highway is only for those who make a choice to seek purity and holiness continuously throughout the day. Isaiah 35:8 says:

> *And a highway will be there; it will be called the Way of Holiness; it will be for those who walk on that Way. The unclean will not journey on it; wicked fools will not go about on it.*

Recently I was attending a small meeting at a university nearby where a woman named Heidi Baker shared about her life and ministry. She works in Mozambique and has started thousands of churches in the last ten years. You may ask, "What is the secret to her successful ministry?"

Her secret is living a life of holiness in an intimate relationship with Jesus. She admitted that she had been a driven person, working and working until she was completely exhausted and worn out. Finally she came to the end of herself, and in that place of utter dependence, she learned the secret of abiding and spending more time with God. It changed her entire ministry because now she is filled with joy.

As her ministry grows and becomes more and more demanding, Heidi changes her schedule and spends even more time with God. Reversing everything in her schedule, she gives God even more time as the demands increase. Now they have seven thousand churches, twelve ministry bases, and they work in twenty-five countries! And the numbers increase with each passing day. Everything is about God and holiness and loving people.

Heidi exhorted everyone to dedicate their personal life to holiness, learn to worship everywhere, and stay filled with God. This is where you and I will see real fruitfulness. We must learn to worship God daily and even hourly in the splendor of His holiness. We read in 1 Chronicles 16:27-29:

> *Splendor and majesty are before him; strength and joy in his dwelling place. Ascribe to the LORD, O families of nations, ascribe to the LORD glory and strength, ascribe to the LORD the glory due his name. Bring an offering and come before him; worship the LORD in the splendor of his holiness.*

I was impressed with Heidi's life. She learned—in spite of a busy, hectic schedule—to go deeper still. She didn't let anything keep her from going deeper with God.

King David knew about living a holy life and worshipping a holy God. He knew how to go deeper with God even in the midst of a battle. Even during times of war, he sent out his men to sing and praise God for the splendor of His holiness. They went out ahead of the army praising God along the road. What was the final result of doing this unusual act of devotion? They won the battle!

If you and I choose to walk in holiness and praise even in the midst of difficulty, we will win the battles before us. We will have victory as we travel through each day, experiencing an increasing fruitfulness in our personal life. But the only way we can be fruitful is when we sit in the heavenly realms with a holy God. He has all the answers—we can do nothing of any worth on our own—we desperately need God. And so we must abide in the deep places with Him. As we abide through praise and thanksgiving, God defeats our enemies. We read about Jehoshaphat's strategy to defeat his enemies in 2 Chronicles 20:21-22:

> *After consulting the people, Jehoshaphat appointed men to sing to the Lord and to praise him for the splendor of his holiness as they went out at the head of the army, saying: "Give thanks to the Lord, for his love endures forever." As they began to sing and praise, the LORD set ambushes against the men of Ammon and Moab and Mount Seir who were invading Judah, and they were defeated.*

What is our response to God's holiness?

Because God is perfectly holy, meeting Him requires preparation. We must let Him convict us of sinful living. We must examine our hearts and confess our sins on a regular basis. We must make sure our relationships are right with others. We must come before Him in worship and praise.

As we grow in prayer and intercession, let us welcome God's purifying fire in our lives. Let us rejoice in His holiness and our privilege of having a personal relationship with Him. Let us thank Him for His providential care in our lives, and seek to know Him more and more in an ever-increasing measure.

> The closer you get to holy God, the more obvious even your smallest sins become. The more you know of God's character, the more you will realize the need to wash your hands and purify your heart before you can get close to Him. Are you willing for almighty God to make you absolutely pure before Him so that you can enjoy the maximum possible relationship with Him?[4]
> Henry and Richard Blackaby, *Experiencing God Day-by-Day*

The Providential Care of God

The providence of God reaches as far as the realm of prayer. It has to do with everything for which we pray. Nothing is too small for the eye of God, nothing too insignificant for His notice and His care... His care reaches to the smallest things and has to do with the most insignificant matters that concern men. He who believes in the God of providence is prepared to see His hand in all things that come to him and can pray about everything.[5] E. M. Bounds, *E. M. Bounds on Prayer*

Are you tempted to think that God doesn't care or is not in control of some things that happen in your life or those around you?

You may feel that you have prayed and prayed, and still the door is shut. Yet, you know in your heart that God wants to open it. God can open the door and make a way where there is no way. He is in control, and some things are going to take great faith to believe. He notices and cares about the smallest matters in your life. His providence reaches as far as the realm of prayer. If he could make a way for Moses and the children of Israel in an impossible situation, He can make a way for you.

In Exodus 14:13, we see a three-part exhortation that Moses gave the children of Israel. When we practice this, we go deeper in our relationship with God. There is a key to success in seeing and experiencing God's control and deliverance in our circumstances.

- **Fear not.** There is a tendency to fear, doubt, or question when the door is shut and the obstacles seem insurmountable. When life seems out of control, we must not give way to fear and doubt. We read in James 1:17-18: *That man should not think he will receive anything from the Lord; he is a double-minded man, unstable in all he does.* There are 365 exhortations in the Bible to "fear not", one for every day of the year.

- **Stand still.** There is a tendency to look in all other directions for the answer. But the real answer in most cases will be in standing still, holding our ground in prayer, and looking up into the face of God for the answer. Standing still is so hard for us. Yet it is the real key to success in the spiritual realm.

- **See the salvation of the Lord**. There is a tendency to look for other earthly things to be our salvation when the door is shut regarding our circumstances. Perhaps someone else will come to our rescue. Maybe if we do this or that, things will go in our direction. We must realize that ultimately salvation comes from the Lord. He is our deliverer. He is always in control.

> A man of prayer as well as the man of faith in God, Moses was on the ground. This man of prayer, who recognized God in providence, with commanding force, spoke to the people like this: "Fear ye not, stand still, and see the salvation of the Lord" (Exodus 14:13). With this he lifted up his rod, and according to divine command, he stretched his hand over the sea. The waters divided, and the command issued forth, "Speak unto the children of Israel, that they go forward" (v. 15). And Israel went over the sea on dry ground. God had opened a way, and what seemed an impossible emergency was remarkably turned into a wonderful deliverance.[6] E. M. Bounds, *E. M. Bounds on Prayer*

God offers us so much when we pray. He can do immeasurably more than all that we think and ask. He promises us much, yet we so often settle for so little. Stretch your imagination. Think long and hard about what God is offering you.

It's so vast—it's bigger than anything you can imagine.

In May 1982, astronomers saw a solar flare shoot out from the sun. It was so powerful that their instruments could not measure it. These astronomers estimated that in twenty minutes that flare released more energy than there is produced by the earth in a whole year. Imagine a candle compared to that light. Then imagine that the love and power of God is like that flare compared to a small candle. God's love, power, and ability are so great—so incomprehensible. No eye has seen, ear has heard, or mind can image the glory of what God wants to give us.

What does the providence of God mean to us as believers?

"Providence" in Webster's Dictionary means "the care and superintendence which God exercises over his creatures, the act of providing or preparing for future use or application, foresight, timely care particularly active foresight. A belief in divine providence is a source of great consolation to good men."[7]

Another way to think about this is to realize that God is in control of everything—His care is timely—His eyes see everything. He superintends our lives and actively sees beforehand all that concerns us. This should be a source of great comfort and encouragement to us. This should motivate us to recklessly abandon ourselves to an all-knowing, all-seeing God who is in ultimate control.

> Nothing occurs by accident under the superintendence of an all-wiser and perfectly just God. Nothing happens by chance in God's moral or natural government. God is a God of order, a God of law, but nonetheless a superintendent in the interest of His intelligent and redeemed creatures. Nothing can take place without the knowledge of God![8] E. M. Bounds, *E. M. Bounds on Prayer*

Look at these verses that show God's providential care in your life. His providential care is seen in:

- **The smallest details of your life -** God knows and is in control of everything that happens in your life.

  Are not two sparrows sold for a penny? Yet not one of them will fall to the ground apart from the will of your Father. And even the very hairs of your head are all numbered. So don't be afraid; you are worth more than many sparrows (Matthew 10:29-31).

- **The working of all things together for your good -** God cares for the smallest detail of your life.

  And we know that in all things God works for the good of those who love him, who have been called according to his purpose (Romans 8:28).

- **The ability of God to see and remember everything -** God remembers all of your prayers.

  He provides food for those who fear him; he remembers his covenant forever (Psalm 111: 5).

- **The comforting presence of God in your life -** God is with you in the daily activities of your life. He is always there. He sees and knows everything about you.

> *And God said, "I will be with you. And this will be the sign to you that it is I who have sent you"* (Exodus 3:12).

Newscaster Paul Harvey told an amazing story about God's providential care. This story was about thousands of allied prisoners during Word War II, and many of them were Christians. A bomber took off for Kokura, Japan with a deadly cargo of bombs to drop on the city, but clouds covered the target area. Circling for an hour and running out of fuel, they had to leave without fulfilling their mission. They changed course and bombed a secondary target before heading back to Guam.

Later they shockingly discovered that one week before their bombing mission, the Japanese had transferred a large concentration of captured Americans to the city of Kokura. The cloud had protected these prisoners from getting bombed. If the city hadn't been hidden from the bombers, it would have been destroyed. Thousands of Americans would have died. God works behind the scenes in our lives, even in every detail. We must learn that He is always in control.[9]

When the going gets hard, it may seem like God is not in control or that He has not heard your prayers. Do not grow weary. Just as God was watching over thousands of prisoners, He is watching over you. Strengthen your spirit in God's Word, and cry out to Him. He is holy; He is your deliverer who can break through any obstacle. Do not give way to fear, stand still in quietness, prayer in faith, and watch His salvation and deliverance.

Know that in spite of circumstantial difficulties, God is in control.

This is only a test of your faith. He can move any cloud on your behalf. He is choosing to take you *deeper still.* Do you and I really know what a wonderful blessing it is to be face-to-face with God where He alone is our deliverer and our salvation? When we have no other escape routes, we have truly come to the place where the supernatural can take over. The problem we often have is that we have squeezed God out of being our only source of deliverance. Let us pray and watch God bring forth our deliverance.

Many times I have been in a place where God had to be my deliverer in certain situations in my life. If He didn't come through, then there was no other way. I have seen God break through again and again.

The street a few yards from my house is called "Providence Road". It is a reminder to me that God is in total control. I choose to say, "Yes" to the providence of God. I choose to fear not, stand still, pray, and see the salvation of God.

Will you agree to the providential care of God in your life as well? Will you choose no other escape routes for yourself but God Himself?

God is in control of your life and destiny. His providential care is active. His care is timely. Prayer brings His providence into action. He is overseeing and directing the affairs of your life, even when things seem contrary. Prayer will open the way before you and will bring God's providence into action. God wants to take you *deeper still* in your relationship with Him.

> Things that come to us from second causes are no surprise to God, nor are they beyond his control. His hand can take hold of them in answer to prayer, and He can make afflictions from whatever quarter they may come, work "for us a far more exceeding weight of glory" (2 Corinthians 4:17). The providence of God goes before his saints, opens the way, removes difficulties, solves problems, and rings deliverance when escape seems hopeless.[10] E. M. Bounds, *E. M. Bounds on Prayer*

Deeper Still Life Application
How to Respond to God's Holiness

This exercise is designed to help you apply a right response to God's holiness. There are several responses we should make when we come into the presence of God in His awesome holiness and providential care. Take time to worship God, meditating on Isaiah 6:1-7 as you begin. Wait upon Him for an hour, prayerfully responding to the following verses, and ask Him to develop these attitudes in your life. They will take you deeper in knowing Him:

- Reverence and Fear - When we meet the infinite, we become aware of our finiteness.

  "Do not come any closer," God said. Take off your sandals, for the place where you are standing is holy ground." Then he said, "I am the God of your father, the God of Abraham, the God of Isaac and the God of Jacob." At this, Moses hid his face, because he was afraid to look at God (Exodus 3:5-6).

- A Deep Sense of Sin - Isaiah said, "Woe is me". The Kings James Version used the word "UNDONE". Here was a man who felt he was coming apart. An acquaintance with God should cause us to hate sin.

  "Woe to me!" I cried. "I am ruined! For I am a man of unclean lips, and I live among a people of unclean lips, and my eyes have seen the King, the LORD Almighty" (Isaiah 6:5).

- Awe and Wonder - Wherever God's presence is felt, men encounter the wonder and mystery of His holiness.

  How awesome is the LORD Most High, the great King over all the earth! (Psalm 47:2).

- Seeking God's Presence - When we encounter a holy God, it causes us to become hungry for His presence. We are willing to sacrifice our time so we can seek Him more.

  Look to the LORD and his strength; seek his face always (Psalm 105:4).

- Praise and Worship - Our lives take on a greater dimension of praise and worship. We begin to thank Him for the little details in our lives. We begin to let worship permeate our lives all day.

  Ascribe to the LORD the glory due his name; worship the LORD in the splendor of his holiness (Psalm 29:2).

How to Help Others Respond to God's Holiness

Get together with an individual or group and spend time before the Lord in worship. You may want to review this chapter together as a group. Read Isaiah 6:1-7, and take some time to respond to these verses. As you wait upon Him, prayerfully meditate on the responses to God's holiness together with the verses in this life application. Pray as a group, asking God to develop these attitudes in your lives. Ask God to take you deeper in knowing Him. Close with the following prayer.

My Prayer to God

Lord, take me deeper in knowing You. I pray that you would establish Your reign in my heart. Teach me about Your holiness. Teach me to seek Your presence all throughout the day. I seek to walk along the highway of holiness. Remove from my life that which is not of You. I desire Your ways in my life, and I stand in awe and wonder at Your holiness and majesty. I long to praise and worship You with my entire life. Purify me so that I might enjoy the fullness of my relationship with You. Make Your dwelling place in my heart. Let everything I do and say glorify Your name, and make me a blessing to others.

Thank you that I can partner with you in order to see the release of Your divine will on earth, the summing up of all things in You. I praise you for your acts of power and for your surpassing greatness (Psalm 150:2). I thank You for taking me deeper still in knowing You and Your holiness. I will ascribe to the LORD the glory due his name; I worship You in the splendor of Your holiness (Psalm 29:2). In Jesus' name, amen.

CHAPTER TWO

DEEPER IN GLORIFYING CHRIST

For in Christ all the fullness of the Deity lives in bodily form,
and in Christ you have been brought to fullness.
He is the head over every power and authority.
Colossians 2:9

THE MUSIC BEGINS, and in breath-taking beauty she begins to walk down the aisle holding tightly to her father's arm. She has carefully planned months for this moment, and all her life she has dreamed of what it would be like and imagined how she would feel.

All eyes are fixed on the glowing radiance of this bride as she shyly steps forth into a brand new life. The bridegroom stands resolutely in front with eyes penetratingly fixed on his young bride. He is a King adorned with great royalty, a lover beyond all lovers, and forever captivated by her beauty. All else fades into the background as he sees her for the first time in her beautiful white wedding gown fashioned especially for his eyes and his pleasure.

Each one of us has been enchanted many times with the wondrous beauty of a wedding. Each bride seems to be radiant and majestic as she walks down the aisle in her gorgeous white gown carrying her bouquet of beautiful, colorful, and sweet-smelling flowers carefully chosen for that special day. Yet, not one of us has fully grasped the reality that we are the Bride of Christ preparing for our future wedding day.

If we truly understood this, it would affect everything in our life—how we live, how we love, and how we walk through our daily life circumstances. If we could only understand that we are preparing to marry our Bridegroom King, it would change our countenance and even how we pray and intercede. If we knew what it really meant to be marrying a majestic and glorious King—who is supreme above all kings and greater than all others—we would live in another dimension.

God wants to open our eyes to this reality. Jesus is our Bridegroom King. He is head over every power and authority. This great and glorious King is loving and compassionate. He is worthy of our highest praise.

This chapter is about growing deeper in glorifying Christ. You may ask, "How can I know the greatness of Christ in a deeper way? How can I celebrate His supremacy and make Him my all in all? Is there a way that I can prepare to marry this Bridegroom King?"

Let God open your eyes to the supremacy of Christ, and learn afresh how to celebrate His greatness. Let's learn to make Jesus our one thing, our highest devotion. This is one of the secrets to a deeper prayer life. Discover how He is our greatest intercessor.

The Supremacy of Christ

The Son is the image of the invisible God, the firstborn over all creation. For in him all things were created: things in heaven and on earth, visible and invisible, whether thrones or powers or rulers or authorities; all things have been created through him and for him. He is before all things, and in him all things hold together. And he is the head of the body, the church; he is the beginning and the firstborn from among the dead, so that in everything he might have the supremacy (Colossians 1:15-18).

If we want a powerful prayer life, we must believe that Christ is supreme and above all. This needs to go much deeper than head knowledge. It needs to be heart revelation. We need to abide in this truth. It is important to have a high view of Christ; He is our representative, advocate, our intercessor, Bridegroom, King, and Savior. Jesus is supreme in our prayer life. We pray in His powerful name—we glorify and worship Him throughout the day—we intercede to the supreme Christ who is Head over all, the majestic Savior of the world, and our Bridegroom King. This knowledge of the supremacy of Christ should affect us in every way. It should radically affect our prayer life.

We live in a world that tries to minimize the supremacy of Christ. Satan knows that his time is short. The antichrist spirit is permeating society in every area. If we are bringing the Kingdom of God and Christ into this world through our prayers, we must know and proclaim the power of this truth—the reality of the supremacy of Christ over every area of darkness encountered on earth.

This truth is found in Colossians 3:11b: *but Christ is all, and is in all.* Let the inner knowledge of the supremacy of Christ touch you deeply. Let this staggering reality change your life completely. May it touch all who are growing in intercession as Christ's disciples just as it did the Apostles Peter, Paul, and John. Francis Frangipane, intercessor and author of *Holiness, Truth and the Presence of God,* wrote:

> But the reality of God is staggering! Peter did not succumb under the convicting power of "religious knowledge"—he met the reality of Jesus Christ! On the road to Damascus, Paul was not blinded and devastated by a "new doctrine"—he met the reality of Jesus Christ! When John beheld our glorified Lord on Patmos, it was not a "new spiritual insight" that left him slain as a dead man—he beheld Jesus Christ![1]

What Does His Supremacy Mean in His Name?

- **Lord** (Kurios). He is Lord, master, and owner.

- **Jesus** (Iesous). He is Yahweh. Yahweh is help and salvation.

- **Christ** (Kristos). He is the Anointed One, a title for Messiah.

- **The Lord Jesus Christ.** He is our master, owner, the God who brings us salvation. He is the Anointed one.

Notice how the Scriptures present His supremacy in Philippians 2:8-11:

> *And being found in appearance as a man, he humbled himself by becoming obedient to death—even death on a cross! Therefore God exalted him to the highest place and gave him the name that is above every name, that at the name of Jesus every knee*

*should bow, in heaven and on earth and under the earth, and
every tongue acknowledge that Jesus Christ is Lord, to the glory
of God the Father.*

Take time to sit and meditate on the following verses. Worship Jesus in
His supremacy, glory, and greatness. As you worship Him and pray
these verses, He will seem bigger in your eyes:

- **He is the image of the invisible God, the representation of
  the reality of God.** He is the absolutely authentic representation of God's being.

  *The Son is the radiance of God's glory and the exact representa-
  tion of his being, sustaining all things by his powerful word. After
  he had provided purification for sins, he sat down at the right
  hand of the Majesty in heaven* (Hebrews 1:3).

- **He is the firstborn over all creation.** Firstborn means His
  lordship, dignity, excellence, and leadership of all creation.

  *The Son is the image of the invisible God, the firstborn over all
  creation* (Colossians 1:15).

- **He is the Creator and sustainer of all things.** Through Him
  all things were made. He is the author and dispenser of light,
  life, and salvation. He is supreme over all.

  *In the beginning was the Word, and the Word was with God, and
  the Word was God. He was with God in the beginning. Through
  him all things were made; without him nothing was made that has
  been made. In him was life, and that life was the light of all mankind* (John 1:1-4).

- **He is the head of the Church.** Jesus Christ should have the
  supreme rank in our lives because he is the head of the body,
  the Church.

  *And he is the head of the body, the church; he is the beginning and
  the firstborn from among the dead, so that in everything he might
  have the supremacy* (Colossians 1:18).

- **He is seated in the place of absolute authority.**

> *Since, then, you have been raised with Christ, set your hearts on things above, where Christ is, seated at the right hand of God* (Colossians 3:1).

- **He is called God by God.**

  > *But about the Son he says, "Your throne, O God, will last for ever and ever; a scepter of justice will be the scepter of your kingdom. You have loved righteousness and hated wickedness; therefore God, your God, has set you above your companions by anointing you with the oil of joy"* (Hebrews 1:8-9).

Jesus Christ is victor! Some theologians illustrate this important truth through the following story.

If a city were under siege, the enemy surrounding it would not let anyone out. Supplies would run low and the citizens would fear for their lives. Imagine in the darkness of night, a spy sneaking in through the enemy lines. He rushes to the city to tell the people that in another place the enemy force has been completely defeated. Everyone has surrendered and the battle has been won. The people do not have to fear because in a matter of time, the besieging troops would hear the news and lay down their weapons.

Many times we feel surrounded by forces of darkness. It comes to us through injustice, disease, oppression, death, and numerous other ways. But the truth is that the enemy has already been defeated when Jesus died on the cross. Things are really not the way they seem. It is only a matter of time until everyone sees that the battle is over.[2]

As intercessors, we need to lift our view of Christ higher and higher.

- See His greatness in your life situation.
- See His ability to answer your prayers.
- See His solution to every problem you face.

The devil is doing all he can to destroy the reality of Christ's supremacy. He is trying to convince the world that he has won. But the truth of the matter is this—the greatest battle has already been won at the cross. Jesus Christ is the answer to the world, He is the reason for our existence, and He is our help in every circumstance. He is the living Christ, the head of the Church, but most of us do not realize the riches we have in Him.

One cold day the body of a sixty-year-old man named Timothy Henry Gray was found by children sledding under a railroad overpass in Wyoming. It appeared that he died of hypothermia. His siblings told NBC News reporters that he disappeared in 1990 without a word.

Timothy Gray was an adopted great-grandson of former U.S. Senator William Andrews Clark, known as one of the copper kings of Montana. Clark was a banker, builder of railroads, and the founder of Las Vegas. Clark's youngest daughter, Huguette Clark, was heiress to the copper mining fortune but died in 2011 in New York City at age 104. She was a recluse who spent more than twenty years living in New York hospitals with a collection of dolls.

Gray was her half great-nephew and the potential heir to her fortunes. If the relatives won the court case, Gray's estate would be entitled to about $19 million before taxes or 6.25 percent of Clark's copper mining fortune, estimated at $307 million. Timothy Gray was not using the money he already had, and the coroner said his wallet contained a cashier's check for a significant amount.

This elderly man was living homeless under a railroad overpass in the cold—as if he had nothing. Yet, he was a millionaire! His life could have been so much different. Likewise, you and I have so many riches in Christ, yet so many of us are living like this homeless man. We live as beggars when God has so much for us.

As we abide in Him and in the reality of His glorious supremacy, we become partakers of His resurrection life—His victorious life. Jesus Christ is our greatest intercessor. We are His glorious Bride, just as we saw in the wedding illustration at the beginning of this chapter. As we follow Him and pray in His name, we pray in His authority. We begin to see His power over sin and over every spiritual battle we face. We begin to rise up to our destiny in Christ because we are seated with Him in heavenly places—and we know it! (Colossians 3:1; Eph. 2:6).

> He who abides in Christ the Risen and Glorified One, becomes in the same way partaker of His resurrection life and of the glory with which He has now been crowned in heaven. Unspeakable are the blessings that flow to the soul from the union with Jesus

in His glorified life. This life is a life of perfect victory and rest... Abiding in Jesus, in whom he has been raised and set in the heavenly places, he receives of that glorious life streaming from the Head through every member of the body.[3] Andrew Murray, *Andrew Murray on Prayer*

Christ—The Greatest Intercessor

How enthroned, magnificent, and royal the intercession of our Lord Jesus Christ at His Father's right hand in heaven! The benefits of His intercession flow to us through our intercessions. Our intercession ought to catch by contagion and by necessity the inspiration and largeness of Christ's great work at His Father's right hand. His business and His life are to pray. Our business and our lives ought to be to pray, and to "pray without ceasing" (1 Thessalonians 5:17).[4] E. M. Bounds, *E. M. Bounds on Prayer*

When you run out of strength and motivation to pray, look at the greatest intercessor throughout all of history—the Lord Jesus Christ. He is always interceding for us. If this is the ministry He is involved in, surely this should help us to continue in his example and not give up.

He is our intercessor; we are partners with Him in intercession. Jesus is presently seated at the Father's right hand with unlimited power. He wants us to share in this mighty work of intercession. Just the thought, that Jesus made prayer His greatest ministry while on earth, should motivate and challenge us to lay hold of this great and powerful ministry. Understanding this is one of the secrets to a deeper prayer life. Jesus has gone deeper in prayer than any of us can imagine. Our Bridegroom is leading us in intercession. The power of heaven is at our disposal!

Christ—The Greatest Intercessor on Earth

In his life on earth Christ began His work as intercessor. Think of the high-priestly prayer on behalf of His disciples and of all who should through them believe in His name. Think of His word to Peter, "I have prayed for thee, that thy faith fail not"

(Luke 22:32): a proof of how intensely personal His intercession is. And on the cross He spoke as intercessor: "Father, forgive them" (Luke 23:34).[5] Andrew Murray, *Andrew Murray on Prayer*

The Scripture leaves no question about the incarnation of Christ. God became human. When Jesus Christ walked on earth He had all the limitation of a real human being: He ate, got tired, wept, suffered, and was tempted. It appears that as a real man He used none of His Godhead powers directly for the entire duration of His earthly ministry. He did all that a true trusting son of a father would do. Jesus demonstrated all the characteristics of true humanity without sinning. And yet, while on earth and in His humanity, Jesus was the greatest intercessor.

In looking at His earthly life, there are many examples that point to the great emphasis he put on prayer and intercession. In His farewell discourse He assures us seven times that He will do what we ask Him. The following are some examples that should motivate each one of us to a greater life of intercession. It should challenge us to go *deeper still* in the ministry of prayer. Let's learn from His example. Let's never forget that Christ was the greatest intercessor on earth:

- **He prayed before He began His public ministry.** When He did this, God opened heaven and empowered Jesus with the Holy Spirit. Likewise, our public ministry is only as powerful as our prayer life. See Luke 3:21-22.

- **He emphasized prayer in His teaching.** He emphasized prayer in His Sermon on the Mount. He often spoke about prayer on other occasions. We also should encourage others to pray. See Mathew 6:5-13; Luke 6:28; 18:1.

- **He trained His disciples to pray.** He took Peter, James, and John with Him up into the mountains to pray. He often prayed together with His disciples. Mentoring others in prayer is a vital ministry for every intercessor. See Luke 9:28-29.

- **He prayed for direction.** Before choosing the twelve disciples, Jesus spent the entire night in prayer. He sought God for direction always and did not do anything outside the Father's will. We also will receive divine perspective when we pray to God. See Luke 6:12-13.

- **He prayed in secret.** He often withdrew to lonely places to pray. He often got up early in the morning to pray. When we pray in secret, the Father rewards us. See Luke 5:16; Mark 1:35.

- **He prayed in public.** Jesus prayed in public in the midst of His teaching. He was not afraid to pray in public at the Holy Spirit's prompting. He prayed publicly before raising Lazarus. None of us as intercessors should be afraid to pray publicly or in a prayer meeting. See John 11:41-42; 12:28b.

Jesus knows everything about what it is to be human. He went through the storms of life while He was on earth.

I read about an English painter who was invited to an artist's studio to see a picture of a storm at sea. When he saw it, he exclaimed:

"It's absolutely wonderful! It's realistic. How did you ever do it?"

The artist told him, "I went to the coast of Holland and had a fisherman take me out to sea in a storm. I asked him to bind me to the mast and steer right into the storm. The storm was so powerful that I wanted to go to the bottom of the boat, but I couldn't. I was bound to the mast. I was facing that ferocious storm head-on, and I felt it. It blew right through me until it almost became part of me. It was a terrible storm. Afterwards I went to my studio and painted this picture."

Just as this artist could paint such a beautiful and realistic picture because he became like part of a raging sea, so Jesus can feel and understand all that we go through because he became like us in our humanity. Jesus has paid the price to intercede. He has all authority and knows how to pray in our defense. He is our great high priest and is seated at the right hand of the Father who always lives to intercede for us (Romans 8:34).

Christ—The Greatest Intercessor in Heaven

Just think what this means: all His saving work is still carried on in heaven, just as on earth, in unceasing communication with, and direct intercession to, the Father, who is All in All. Every act of grace in Christ has been preceded by, and owes its power to, intercession. God has been honored and acknowledged as its

Author. On the throne of God, Christ's highest fellowship with the Father, and His partnership in the Father's rule of the world, is in intercession. Every blessing that comes down to us from above bears this stamp of God: through Christ's intercession.[6]
Andrew Murray, *Andrew Murray on Prayer*

Jesus Christ is interceding for us in heaven. He is exalted above the heavens. He is our perfect High Priest forever. We will never be without a priestly representative. He will always meet our needs. We read in Hebrews 7:25-26:

Therefore he is able to save completely those who come to God through him, because he always lives to intercede for them. Such a high priest truly meets our need—one who is holy, blameless, pure, set apart from sinners, exalted above the heavens.

His desire for us is that we follow Him. He has paid the price so that we may come to the throne of grace with our intercession and be heard on high. The following truths about the heavenly position of Christ, the greatest intercessor in heaven, should encourage and motivate us to intercede:

- **He is seated at the Father's right hand.** He is exalted to the highest place next to the Father. Because of this, we can pray the will of heaven into the earth realm. When we pray God's will in Jesus' name, our prayers are heard in heaven where Jesus is seated, and He answers our prayers. See Philippians 2:9; Acts 7:55; and Hebrews 1:13.

- **He has all authority.** At the name of Jesus every knee shall bow in heaven, on earth, and under the earth. He is crowned with glory and honor, and everything is put under His feet. He is able to win every battle we bring before Him in prayer because He has all authority in heaven and on earth. See Hebrews 2:7-9 and Philippians 2:9-11.

- **He has paid the price to intercede.** He humbled Himself and became obedient to death on a cross. He gave Himself as a sacrifice for the sins of the world. In light of this great sacrifice, can we not give ourselves to intercession here on earth for His glory? See Hebrews 5:7 and Philippians 2:6-8.

- **He is a great High Priest.** He has gone through the heavens and is able to sympathize with our weakness because He has been tempted in every way like us and, yet, without sin. We can approach the throne of grace with confidence in prayer. See Hebrews 3:1; 4:14-16; 6:20; 7:26.

- **He prays without ceasing.** He always lives to intercede for us. He is our example. The Bible emphasizes continual prayer. Therefore, we should learn to permeate our entire lives with prayer. See Hebrews 7:25 and 1 Thessalonians 5:17.

- **He prays in our defense.** He speaks to the Father in our defense as the Righteous One. He is holy, blameless, pure, and set apart. Therefore, He can pray in our defense when we sin. See 1 John 2:1.

Realize the fact that you are a partner with Jesus Christ in intercession.

He is our head in heaven praying, and we are His body praying on earth. There is an authority in this powerful ministry of intercession. It must become our one great aim in life. Everything else we do will have anointing and power when it is united with intercession. Our intercession will bless the world and glorify God, preparing the world for Christ's return.

Intercession will break through our most difficult trials. Intercession is the key that will unlock the treasures of God on earth. It will open up heaven and bring it to earth. God's perfect will in heaven can only be brought to earth through the ministry of intercession.

Can we consecrate ourselves afresh to this great ministry? Can we make a commitment to prioritize it in our lives? It's time to go *deeper still* in the ministry of prayer. It is time to show earth the power of intercession!

> And now this Christ, the Intercessor, is our life. He is our Head and we are His body. His Spirit and life breathe in us. On earth, as in heaven, intercession is God's chosen, God's only, channel of blessing. Let us learn from Christ what glory there is in it, what the way to exercise this wondrous power is, and what part it is to take in our work for God... By it, beyond anything, we glo-

rify God. By it we glorify Christ. By it we bring blessing to the church and the world. By it we obtain our highest nobility—the godlike power of saving men.[7] Andrew Murray, *Andrew Murray on Prayer*

Christ is All

In the eternal counsel of God, in the redemption on the cross, as King on the throne in heaven and on earth, Christ is all! In the salvation of sinners, in their justification and sanctification, in the up-building of Christ's Body, in the care for individuals, even the most sinful, this world prevails, Christ is all. Every day and every hour, it affords comfort and strength to the child of God, who accepts it in faith: Christ is all.[8] Andrew Murray, *Andrew Murray on Prayer*

As you enter into this day, meditate on the reality that: "Christ is all!" This truth should keep you steady in the midst of change, focused in the midst of so many options, and rejoicing even in the midst of pain.

Last night we were listening to some youthful Christian music where the singer kept singing over and over again, "You are my One Thing." As we went to bed my husband said, "That phrase keeps running through my head." Right now as I write this, there is a conference that thousands of young people are attending called The OneThing Conference. The truth is that Jesus Christ is our one thing; He is everything. We must keep this continually before us on a daily basis:

"You are my One Thing. You are my all!"

Both history and humanity point to the fact that Christ is of supreme importance and that He is all. Meditate with a sense of deep awe on the following facts:

- No one was born like He was.

- No one spoke like He did.

- No one could do what He did.

- No one could claim absolute innocence like He did.

- No one ever humbled himself as He did.

- No one died like He did.

- No one rose from the dead like He did.

- No one's fame increased after his death as His did.

- No one has changed the lives of so many people as He has.

- No one changed history like He has.

The word "supremacy" in Noah's Dictionary gives this definition: "State of being supreme or in the highest station of power, highest authority, holding the highest place in government or power, highest, greatest or most excellent, in the highest degree, to the utmost extent, over, above and beyond."[9] Jesus Christ has the highest authority. Philip Shaft expands the greatness and supremacy of Christ in these words:

> This Jesus of Nazareth, without money and arms, conquered more millions than Alexander, Caesar, Mohammed, and Napoleon; without science and learning, He shed more light on things human and divine than all the philosophers and scholars combined; without the eloquence of schools, He spoke such words of life as were never spoken before or since, and produced effects which lie beyond the reach of orator of poet; without writing a single line, He set more pens in motion, volumes, works of art and songs of praise than the whole army of great men of ancient and modern times.[10]

Humanity presents his greatness in the following ways:

- **Proof of His followers.** Of the twelve men that He discipled, eleven were martyrs on the basis of two things: The resurrection and their belief in Him as the Son of God.

- **Proof of His enemies.** Christ is often portrayed as being a little baby in a manger or a poor weak man hanging on a cross, and the devil has done all he can to mar the truth of what He really is. But, even Satan cannot keep the greatness of the supremacy of Christ a secret.

- **Proof of the world.** He was a good man, a good teacher, and a good prophet and religious leader. Even the world testifies to His greatness. His life was without flaw.

We must pray that the reality of the supremacy of Christ would affect His Church worldwide. See Ephesians 1:17-21 for a wonderful way to pray for wisdom and revelation for the Church. We must pray that Christ is all and that "You are my One Thing" is true for each one of us. This is more important than any of us can presently comprehend. We must go *deeper still* in comprehending this truth in our lives. We must pray this reality into the life of every Christian. We read in Ephesians 1:22-23:

> *And God placed all things under his feet and appointed him to be head over everything for the church, which is his body, the fullness of him who fills everything in every way.*

Jesus Christ holds the highest place.

> *Therefore God exalted him to the highest place and gave him the name that is above every name, that at the name of Jesus every knee should bow, in heaven and on earth and under the earth, and every tongue acknowledge that Jesus Christ is Lord, to the glory of God the Father* (Philippians 2:9-11).

Deeper Still Life Application
How to Celebrate the Supremacy of Christ

Take some time to review this chapter prayerfully. Carefully meditate on Ephesians 1:17-21, praying these verses daily for the Church. Meditate on other Scriptures presented here. Praise, thank, and pray every day this week for the following:

- Worship Jesus Christ for His position of supreme authority in Ephesians 1:20-21 - Christ is the supreme Ruler over all rulers, the supreme King over all kingdoms, and the supreme Governor over all governments. Pray that all believers would realize this. See Philippians 3:20 and Psalm 103:19.

- Pray that believers would comprehend the magnitude of what it means that "Christ is all" - This revelation cannot come by natural reasoning or by head knowledge. Christ's authority is now supreme over the universe and that same power that raised Christ to that position of authority now works in us who believe.

- Praise Jesus that He rules now in the midst of his enemies - Christ's Kingdom is supreme. Jesus rules by "the rod of His strength" (Psalm 110:2). The rod marks His authority. We exercise His authority in His name through our prayers. This is how we advance His Kingdom.

- Pray that believers would live out the reality of Christ's supremacy in their daily lives - Pray that "You are my One Thing" becomes true for the entire body of Christ. Pray that it becomes true in your own life.

- Praise God that it is His purpose to share the authority of His kingdom with His people - Pray that all Christians worldwide would understand and lay hold of the reality of Christ's Kingdom. We are made alive, raised up, and enthroned in the heavenly Kingdom. This is the position He shares with us. Pray Ephesians 2:4-6 over the Church.

- Pray that believers worldwide would know their position in Christ at God's right hand - Pray that they would understand their rights and responsibilities as citizens of heaven. Pray that God's Spirit would reveal this to each one of us. See 1 Corinthians 2:9-10.

Write a prayer to the Lord celebrating His supremacy in your life. Use Scripture in your prayer, and end with praying "My Prayer to God."

How to Help Others·
Celebrate the supremacy of Christ

Get together with an individual or group and review this chapter. Read all the Scriptures in this life application, taking time to comment on each one. Then have a good time of praise and prayer for the requests on the previous page. You may want to type out these prayer points with the verses included for personal prayer and meditation during the week. Close with the following prayer. This week have each individual write a prayer, celebrating the supremacy of Christ in their personal life.

My Prayer to God

Lord, I praise You that You are supreme and above all. You are the image of the invisible God (Hebrews 1:3) and the firstborn over all creation (Colossians 1:15). You are the sustainer of all things (John 1:1-4) and seated in the place of absolute authority. Thank You for sharing the authority of Your Kingdom with me. I am made alive, raised up, and enthroned in the heavenly Kingdom with You (Ephesians 2:4-6). Reveal this to my heart in a deeper way. You were the greatest intercessor while you lived on earth. You prayed before ministry, in private, in public, and throughout the whole night. You are ever living to intercede for me now. You are seated at the Father's right hand praying. Help me to know my position at your right hand (1 Cor. 2:9-10). You are my great High Priest.

Reveal to my heart the importance of prayer, and give me a burning heart to exercise the wondrous power of prayer for your glory and for the salvation of souls. I want to understand my bridal identity and know You as my Bridegroom King. You are my One Thing. You are the supreme Ruler over all rulers, the su-

preme King over all kingdoms, and the supreme Governor over all governments. You rule now in the midst of Your enemies. Your Kingdom is supreme. I praise You for Your supremacy in my life. In Jesus' name, amen.

CHAPTER THREE

⊰⊱

DEEPER IN PARTNERING
WITH THE HOLY SPIRIT

In the same way, the Spirit helps us in our weakness.
We do not know what we ought to pray, but the Spirit
himself intercedes for us with groans that words cannot express.
And he who searches our hearts knows the mind of the Spirit,
because the Spirit intercedes for the saints
in accordance with God's will.
Romans 8:26-27

⊰⊱

OUR NEIGHBOR URGENTLY APPROACHED US and said:

"Rich was in a motorcycle accident! He is in a coma in the hospital. Will you come and pray for him?"

We had a tradition of prayer walking our neighborhood. It was during one of these walks where we suddenly learned the sad news that our neighbor, Rich, was struck by a car, while riding his motorcycle and was in a coma with severe life-threatening injuries. This news sent us immediately to the hospital where we entered a lonely room where Rich's lifeless body was lying. The only sign of life was the twitching of his eyelids.

Two other neighbors joined us at the hospital. We spoke the gospel to this lifeless man. Maybe he could hear our words of hope as he lay silently inside that body. By faith we spoke words of life and healing in the name of Jesus. Then we put a few drops of oil on his head. We didn't know how to pray to someone in a coma, but the Holy Spirit helped us in our weakness. We were partnering with Him. We simply prayed for Rich's healing. We asked the Holy Spirit to heal his broken body.

Then we left not knowing what would happen.

A few days after we had prayed, the hospital staff was stunned to see our neighbor rise out of bed. He said he was hungry. Several days later, he was released under observation but when we saw him, he said he felt fine. I asked him, "Rich, what does this mean to you?" He immediately responded, "This is a wake-up call for me!"

Another neighbor who knew of our ministry to him stopped in front of our house and said, "The doctors are wondering what happened, but we know, don't we?" After that several neighbors came to the Lord.

The Holy Spirit is able to perform miracles. He helps us in our weakness. He helps us in our prayers. The Holy Spirit worked in Rich's life and brought healing. Rich has moved from our neighborhood, but we know that the Holy Spirit is working in his life as well as others through that experience.

You may wonder, "How can I partner with the Holy Spirit and see God work through my prayers? How do I pray for the lost?" In this chapter learn about the ministry and power of the Holy Spirit. Discover how the Holy Spirit is working in the world and how to go deeper in partnering in prayer with Him.

The Holy Spirit and Prayer

The Holy Spirit descending from Christ to us draws us up into the great stream of His ascending prayers. The Spirit prays for us without words in the depth of a heart where even thoughts are at times formless. He takes us up into the wonderful flow of the life of the triune God. Through the Spirit, Christ's prayers become ours, and ours are made His. We ask for what we desire, and it is given to us."[1] Andrew Murray, *Andrew Murray on Prayer*

The power of the Holy Spirit is a vital necessity in our prayer life. He is the key to a life of intercession. Partnering with Him in prayer will change our prayer life. We cannot attempt to pray great prayers without acknowledging His vital presence in our life. We cannot know how to pray effectively without the wisdom and understanding of the Holy Spirit. In my experience in prayer, both personally and corporately, I have experienced the spirit of prayer released in a most powerful way when the Holy Spirit enters the prayer meeting. Let us welcome Him daily and pray:

Come, Holy Spirit. Lead me and guide me in my prayer time. Pray through me. Have your way in my life.

We must grab hold of the reality of who the Holy Spirit is and what He means in our lives, specifically in our prayer lives. This is one of the secrets to a deeper prayer life. It will not work to have a hurried, microwave approach to the Holy Spirit. He wants our time. He wants to show us Who He is and what He can do through our prayers.

As the body of Christ, we have caused division over issues regarding the Holy Spirit. As the Church worldwide, we have not fully understood the power of the Holy Spirit. One day we will, and it will change everything we do because we will really know what it means to have God living in us.

A lady went to a jeweler to get her watch fixed. He disappeared and came back quickly with her watch running perfectly. She asked him, "How could you fix it in such a short time?" He told her that it only needed a small battery. All this time the lady had been trying to wind the watch. She didn't know she only needed a battery to keep it running.

This is so much like the Christian life. Many times we do not realize the inner power that we have in the Holy Spirit. The Holy Spirit can run everything in our life, but so often we think we have to take matters into our own hands. So we live a powerless life. The lack of reality, godliness, power, and fruit in our lives is due to the unbelief or improper understanding of the Holy Spirit. We need to go deeper in partnership with the Holy Spirit if we want to live powerful lives.

The longer I am a Christian, the more I am discovering the friendship of the Holy Spirit in my life and my desperate need of Him daily. I can't do anything without Him. Whenever I have been in deep distress or difficulty, I have cried out to God with all my heart. In times of crisis, I have personally experienced the Holy Spirit's comfort. I am sure you can agree when you think about times of difficulty when you needed God's intervention.

One of the first things we must acknowledge is that the Holy Spirit is a person, the third person of the Trinity, who lives within us.

He is referred to as a person in John 16:13-14. This is a powerful reality. We are not alone in our prayers. The Spirit is not an impersonal force but a real person living inside of us. This is life-changing if we can only grasp its significance. And He is God. He is the Spirit (pnuema), and this means: "wind, breath, spirit, immaterial, and powerful". He is holy. This means that He is set apart, righteous, and pure. The Holy Spirit can be like the wind that is invisible, immaterial, and powerful.

The Holy Spirit has personal characteristics. He searches, grieves, works, talks, teaches, and helps. He is divine, eternal (Hebrews 9:14), and is everywhere present (Psalm 139:7-10). He has foreknowledge, is omniscience (Acts 1:16), and was involved in creation (Genesis 1:2; Psalm 104:30). We must not overlook the personhood of the Holy Spirit and His great provision for the Church. He is described in so many excellent ways!

Meditate on these wonderful descriptions of the Holy Spirit. Apply these descriptions personally to your own life. Think about it. What does this mean to you in your daily walk? How should this affect your prayer life?

- The Spirit of life - Revelation 11:11.

- The Spirit of holiness - Romans 1:4.

- The Spirit of wisdom - Ephesians 1:17; Isaiah 11:2.

- The Spirit of faith - 2 Corinthians 4:13.

- The Spirit of truth - John 14:17.

- The Spirit of grace - Hebrews 10:29.

- The Spirit of supplication - Zechariah 12:10.

- The Spirit of adoption - Romans 8:15.

- The Spirit of power, love and self-discipline - 2 Timothy 1:7.

The river that flows from the throne of God is the Spirit, and Jesus said that out of your innermost being shall flow rivers of living water (John 7:38). In John 3:8 and Acts 2:2, the Spirit is described as the sound of a violent, rushing wind. My husband, Norm, is from Buffalo, New York where Niagara Falls is located. We often visit the falls and are always amazed at that violent, gushing waterfall. It is powerful and sounds like the violent, rushing wind.

An author named Jamie Buckingham visited a dam on the Columbia River. He thought that the water spilling over the top gave the dam its' power, but he was absolutely wrong. That was only the froth. The turbines and generators deep within transformed the power of tons and tons of water into electricity. All of this was happening quietly and without notice deep within.

In the same way, it is the Holy Spirit who is working deep within each of our lives. He gives us the power. It isn't the flashy froth like in this dam, but it is His deep work in our lives that gives us real spiritual power and makes us like a river of living water.

Sometimes as intercessors we just want more of God, but we may feel alone or even abandoned. Very few might show up to the prayer meeting, or we may be wrestling with our own personal trials. When this happens, realize that you are never alone; this wonderful Holy Spirit cares and is living within you. He knows every single detail of your life. He will never abandon you. You may grieve or quench Him, but He will not let you go. He is for you—he is so interested in blessing your life and helping you.

- Can you believe that?

- Can you begin to grasp how deeply He wants to help you to grow as a Christian and use you in His Kingdom purposes?

- Can you begin to know how deeply He feels for you in every joy or sorrow you face?

The Holy Spirit is personal, and He is always available to you. It is important for you to believe that He will help you in your prayer life. He wants to partner with you. He wants to take you *deeper still* in your prayer life. He can take hold of situations with you and add His strength to yours.

In situations where we're experiencing difficulty in obtaining results, the Holy Spirit wants to take hold of the situation with us, adding His strength to ours. He also wants to help or take hold with us by directing us how to pray "for we know not what we should pray for as we ought" (Romans 8:26 KJV)... Realizing our weaknesses and our inability to produce results causes us to look to Him for help. If we allow Him to pray through us, He will take hold together with us. We just have to believe that when the Holy Spirit takes hold, something is going to move![2] Dutch Sheets, *Watchman Prayer*

The Holy Spirit's Ministry and Power

This is more than the Spirit with a portion of Christ's influence and power. This is the Holy Spirit, the Spirit of the glorified Jesus in His exaltation and power, coming to us as the Spirit of the indwelling Jesus, revealing the Son and the Father within us (John 14:16-23). This Spirit cannot simply be the Spirit of our hours of prayer. It must be the Spirit of our whole lives and walks, glorifying Jesus in us by revealing the completeness of His work and making us wholly one with Him and like Him. Then we can pray in His name, because we are truly one with Him. Then we have the immediate access to the Father of which Jesus said, "I say not unto you, that I will pray the Father for you" (John 16:26).[3] Andrew Murray, *Andrew Murray on Prayer*

Without the Holy Spirit, I can do nothing.

This is a strong statement that I have already mentioned, but it is absolutely true. A serious problem is that the Holy Spirit is left out of so many of our church activities. For many of us, there is no heart knowledge of the ministry and power of the Holy Spirit in every aspect of our Christian life. This must change. We must begin to acknowledge our need of the Holy Spirit just as we acknowledge our need for our every breath. If we were drowning, we would be gasping for air. In a similar way, we are going through turbulent waters and must depend upon the Holy Spirit to carry us through the ruggedness of the end times.

Our life depends on it. We must know His power!

Samuel Shoemaker said this powerful statement, "It must be perfectly obvious to anyone that what the whole church needs from top to bottom is a deeper conversion, a profounder experience of the power of the Holy Spirit."[4]

The Ministry of the Holy Spirit

Jesus depended completely on the power of the Holy Spirit to do the work. When He became man, He laid aside the attributes of His deity. He knew that He could not lean on His own strength. He was absolutely dependent on the Holy Spirit to accomplish the will of God. His ministry began when the Spirit descended on Him like a dove.

We, likewise, cannot do anything to accomplish God's will without the ministry of the Holy Spirit in our lives. There are seven words we can use to describe the Holy Spirit's ministry—Comforter, Helper, Counselor, Advocate, Intercessor, Strengthener, and Standby. The Holy Spirit gives us power to do His work. He gives us the ability to pray and to live a godly life. The Holy Spirit helps us in every area of our life and ministry. He is the key to our success. The Apostle Paul depended on the Holy Spirit to do the work. He said in 1 Corinthians 2:2-5:

> *For I resolved to know nothing while I was with you except Jesus Christ and him crucified. I came to you in weakness with great fear and trembling. My message and my preaching were not with wise and persuasive words, but with a demonstration of the Spirit's power, so that your faith might not rest on human wisdom, but on God's power.*

Meditate on these verses, and see all that the Holy Spirit does in relation to the believer:

- The Holy Spirit regenerates - John 3:3-6.

- The Holy Spirit indwells - Romans 8:11; 1 Corinthians 6:19.

- The Holy Spirit seals - Ephesians 1:13; 4:30.

- The Holy Spirit sanctifies - Romans 8:15.

- The Holy Spirit gives spiritual gifts - 1 Corinthians 12:1-11.

- The Holy Spirit empowers for service - Acts 1:8.

- The Holy Spirit guides - Acts 13:2; 1 Corinthians 2:4.

- The Holy Spirit teaches - 1 John 2:20.

- The Holy Spirit prays - Romans 8:26-27.

Here at the International House of Prayer, we experience the ministry and power of the Holy Spirit in our eight-day training called Immerse. Immerse is perfect for people in ministry, in the workplace, at school, or at home who desire to grow in the knowledge and love of Jesus, experience first-hand a lifestyle of prayer and worship, build friendships with like-minded Christians, and walk in a greater measure of the power of the Holy Spirit. People encounter God in the prayer room, classroom, and at our weekend service and teaching services.

I work with Immerse and love it. It is so amazing to see the Holy Spirit at work every day in the lives of individuals, bringing many into physical and emotional healing. So many are healed and brought into a fresh encounter with the Holy Spirit and intimacy with God. I see the Holy Spirit at work in every dimension, transforming the lives of so many so quickly and giving them exactly what they need. If you would like to know more about Immerse, see www.ihopkc.org/immerse.

The Holy Spirit wants to partner with us in life in a deeper dimension than we have ever experienced before. He wants to have His strength and power operating within us—He wants to give us His wisdom—He wants to participate in everything we are doing. When we pray, He wants to pray with us and through us. He wants to transform everything that we do with His glorious power. Understanding the ministry of the Holy Spirit is a secret to a deeper prayer life.

Transformed by the Power of the Holy Spirit

Over the past five years, God has led us on a journey—away from a "normal" church and into a house of prayer. We now understand that the journey has just begun. The Holy Spirit continues to lead us into new levels of prayer, and new levels of blessing, power, understanding and fruitfulness. It's clear to us that as we offer more prayers, there is more of God... and more of everything."[5] James Graf, "No Longer Normal"

The Holy Spirit is able to transform lives and churches. There is an outstanding testimony from James Graf in his article "No Longer Normal" that tells how the Holy Spirit transformed a bilingual, multiethnic church when they increased their prayer ministry.

A few years ago this church was a normal, traditional church. The leaders began to sense that God wanted to do more if they would seek Him earnestly. They began to pray more intensely as a church. Their church had planned to launch a big building project. During that time the pastor went on a forty-day fast.

Soon they discovered sin in the church leadership, and everything stopped. The Holy Spirit began to deal with the hearts and attitudes of the leadership. He challenged their level of commitment and their comfort zones. A transformation took place after they responded to the conviction of the Holy Spirit. Graf said:

> In response, we began the difficult process of surrendering these things to God. He led us to pray out of weakness and desperation things like, "God, we need You; We can't do anything without You; We're thirsty for more of Your presence; We don't care about the other things we've been focusing on, we just want to know You." He answered those prayers with a transformation of our church which continues to this day."[6]

The transformation process was not easy because not everyone in the church was glad about a greater prayer ministry. Some even left the church. But the leaders kept seeking the presence of God instead of seeking church membership. And God added to their number.

The power of the Holy Spirit was evident even in the midst of uncomfortable change. Individuals would come to the altar weekly in brokenness. Fasting increased in the church, and a new church was planted. The Holy Spirit was welcomed to every gathering. Intercession was greatly increased for their city. Unbelievers were getting saved during the prayer meetings. The city is now coming to the church and asking for help. James Graf gave this remarkable testimony:

> Since the Holy Spirit came to our church, we have seen a large increase in the number of desperate, troubled, and seeking people who visit. We haven't used slick advertisements or special events to attract them. We often have visitors tell us that

"something" just led them to stop at this church. We simply ask for souls, and He sends them to us.[7]

Are we willing for the Holy Spirit to invade our homes, our lives, and our churches like this? Are we willing to go through the transformational process that is necessary for the Holy Spirit to have full reign in our lives and for His ministry to have full expression in our city?

We are no longer living in normal days, and we can no longer do things in a routine, human way. We need to go *deeper still* in partnership with the Holy Spirit. We need the ministry and power of the Holy Spirit to bring forth great fruitfulness in our lives. Can you pray the same prayer this church prayed before God began to bring about transformation?

God, we need You; We can't do anything without You; We're thirsty for more of Your presence; We don't care about the other things we've been focusing on, we just want to know You.

When any church can be brought to the place where they will recognize their need of the Holy Spirit and take their eyes off of all men, and surrender absolutely to the Holy Spirit's control, and give themselves to much prayer for His outpouring, and present themselves as His agents, having stored the Word of God in their hearts and then look to the Holy Spirit to give it power as it falls from their lips, a mighty revival in the power of the Holy Spirit is inevitable.[8] R. A. Torrey, "How to Promote and Conduct a Successful Revival"

The Holy Spirit
and Praying for the Lost

The New Testament portrays each person of the Trinity as deeply involved in our prayers: we approach the Father through the Son and are empowered and guided by the Holy Spirit. The apostles exhort us to pray in the Spirit (Ephesians 6:18, Jude 20), and the key verses explaining the Holy Spirit's role in our prayers are found in Romans 8:26-27: "the Spirit helps us in our weakness. We do not know what we ought to pray for, but the Spirit himself intercedes for us... because the Spirit intercedes for the saints in accordance with God's will."[9] Mel Winger, "Supernatural Prayer Partners"

A supernatural prayer partner!

As you labor faithfully in prayer for the lost, keep in mind that you have a supernatural prayer partner who is helping you. You are never alone as you pray.

Many of you have been praying for years regarding lost family members. We have personally seen several come to Christ through prayer, but it sometimes took years. God worked in some very hard cases as we watched the Holy Spirit remove spiritual blindness one by one. The Holy Spirit is at work in the world and in our families or work environments, even when things seem otherwise. In fact, the lost cannot be reached without the dynamic working of the Holy Spirit in a life.

We've already mentioned that the Holy Spirit helps us in our weakness in our prayers. He shows us who to pray for and how to pray. We cannot pray without the help of the Holy Spirit, because He helps us to hit the mark as we intercede for the lost. Notice the following definition of intercession relating to the Holy Spirit:

> Lexicons show the root idea of this word to be, "to light upon by chance, to meet accidentally." So it expresses a fortuitous and unplanned encounter of two parties. That definition seems pointless unless we take into consideration God's (strategy) for prayer... The Holy Spirit is active in 1) bringing to mind people or circumstances we ought to pray for, and 2) giving rise to prayer that exactly hits the mark. That is, God Himself knows where hearts cry for His intervention, and the Holy Spirit prompts prayer to release the workings of His hand for them.[10]

Light is released as we partner with the Holy Spirit in prayer.

Light is released as an intercessor prays for the lost. Satan's strategies keep people in spiritual darkness so they cannot experience God's forgiveness and love. He uses doubt, deception, confusion, blindness, and so many other things to keep them in the dark. He is a thief and comes to steal and rob people of what they can have in Christ. He is their adversary and enemy (1 Peter 5:8). He does everything he can to keep people in darkness—but we can bring them into the light through our prayers.

Dick Eastman, the International President of Every Home for Christ, had a vision several years ago that displays this truth. He saw a big arena with thousands of people of all ages and races standing before a judge's bench. An angel had a gigantic book—the Book of Life (Revelation 20:12-15). Each person had a list that they brought to the judge. They were intercessors! One older intercessor presented her list with many names. Dick asked the Lord how she could possibly get so many names on her list, and He showed him why.

In this vision he suddenly saw the elderly intercessor on her knees in a village in India near a small hut. A man brought a gospel booklet to the lost man in that dark hut, but he immediately threw it on the table. The intercessor began to fervently pray. As she prayed, the darkness in the hut began to move upward. Instantly the man picked up the booklet, read it, and accepted the Lord into his life. A beam of light suddenly entered the hut and flowed into the man's heart.

The darkness vanished!

The intercessor then put his name on her list and went to another hut to pray. When we pray the darkness vanishes and light comes. This is a visual example of how we can partner with the Holy Spirit in prayer for the salvation of souls.[11]

To date, Every Home for Christ has distributed gospel literature house-to-house to 2.2 billion people in 191 countries. More than 27.8 million decisions for Christ have resulted. God is at work in the hearts of the lost as we partner with the Holy Spirit in prayer. As we partner in prayer, He wants us to reach out to the lost. But, often we fail to be His salt and light to a lost and needy world. Most of us need to be greater lights right where God has planted us.

Let's pray this prayer of repentance. Let's ask God to give us love for the lost and a life of power that convinces those in darkness searching for truth that they desperately need Christ in their lives.

A Prayer of Repentance

Lord, You were a shining light to the generation of people who lived two thousand years ago. They flocked to You because You loved them enough to be with them and to show them the true way to the Father. You have commissioned us to shine with that same love and message, yet we have not.

Even in light of the fact that You have given so much to us and have enriched our lives in every way, we have neglected to give proper attention to something so important to You, "to seek and to save the lost" (Luke 19:10). We confess, Lord, that we have been too busy with life. We have loved our lives in this world to the exclusion of the task for which You keep us in the world. Our concern has not been great enough. Our love has not been hot enough. Our vision of eternity has not been clear enough. We have not believed—we have been cowards—we have turned away busying ourselves with temporal pursuits while our neighbors pass, one by one, into a living and dying hell. We haven't cared enough to intentionally love and pray for them.

Lord, we confess what we are, jars of clay. But You, are the potter. We ask that You remold our hearts after Your own heart. Give us a love that will lead the way, a passion hot as fire, and a faith that no disappointment will tire. Give us love for the lost and a life of power that will convince them of eternity and the claims of Jesus Christ. In Jesus' name, amen.[12] Norm Przybylski

Let us pray that we become more passionate in interceding for the harvest. Let's also pray that each one of us will reach out with a new commitment to love and be a light to those who are lost. God wants to take us *deeper still* in partnership with His Spirit in praying for the lost.

I heard a story about a lighthouse that demonstrates the importance of shining the light. One night the man who took care of the lighthouse became very ill. He couldn't attend the light, and it was very rocky on that coast. The light failed to revolve, and the weather became quite dangerous and stormy. This man's young son climbed up the lighthouse with his lamp, and turned the lantern with his hands all during that stormy night.

In the morning they discovered that two ships with seven hundred souls on board had made it safely to shore because of that revolving lantern. That little boy had faithfully turned the light all night long. He had saved hundreds of lives without even knowing it, just because he had kept the light shining where it could be seen. How we need to be God's light in a dark world.

If you would like to know from the Bible how to receive salvation and the free gift of eternal life, here's how you can receive this gift personally.

How to Find Eternal Life

- **God loves you -** *"This is love: not that we loved God, but that he loved us and sent his Son as an atoning sacrifice for our sins"* (1 John 4:10).

- **You have sinned -** *"For all have sinned and fall short of the glory of God"* (Romans 3:23).

- **The result of sin is death and separation from God -** *"For the wages of sin is death, but the gift of God is eternal life in Christ Jesus our Lord"* (Romans 6:23).

- **Jesus died for your sins -** *"But God demonstrates his own love for us in this: While we were still sinners, Christ died for us"* (Romans 5:8).

- **Jesus is the way to eternal life -** *"Jesus answered, 'I am the way and the truth and the life. No one comes to the Father except through me'"* (John 14:6).

- **Heaven is a free gift -** It can't be earned or deserved. *"For it is by grace you have been saved, through faith—and this not from yourselves, it is the gift of God—not by works, so that no one can boast"* (Ephesians 2:8-9).

- **Receive Jesus today as your Savior -** *"For God so loved the world that he gave his one and only Son, that whoever believes in him shall not perish but have eternal life"* (John 3:16).

Admit that you are a sinner and can't get to heaven yourself. Be willing to turn from your sin. Believe that Jesus died for you on the cross. Through prayer, invite Jesus Christ to come into your life.

"Dear Lord Jesus, I know that I am a sinner and need Your for-giveness. I believe that You died for my sins. Forgive me for my sins and everything I've done wrong in my life. I now invite You to come into my heart and life. I want to trust and follow You as the Lord and Savior of my life. Thank You for the free gift of eternal life. In Your name, amen.

For additional information, see www.intercessorsarise.org.

How The Holy Spirit Works in the World

The whole world is in spiritual darkness (Ephesians 2:1-2), but as we pray and partner with the Holy Spirit, that spiritual darkness is lifted. Until the darkness is removed, the unbeliever cannot see the light. We must deal with the darkness in a supernatural way, and this is through prayer. We must understand the ministry of the Holy Spirit in the lives of lost men and women as we pray:

- **The Holy Spirit convicts.**

  When he comes, he will prove the world to be in the wrong about sin and righteousness and judgment (John 16:8).

- **The Holy Spirit witnesses to Christ.**

  When the Advocate comes, whom I will send to you from the Fa-ther—the Spirit of truth who goes out from the Father—he will testify about me (John 15:26).

- **The Holy Spirit invites individuals to salvation.**

  The Spirit and the bride say, "Come!" And let the one who hears say, "Come!" Let the one who is thirsty come; and let the one who wishes take the free gift of the water of life (Revelation 22:17).

- **The Holy Spirit regenerates.**

  Jesus replied, "Very truly I tell you, no one can see the kingdom of God unless they are born again. "How can someone be born when they are old?" Nicodemus asked, "Surely they cannot enter a se-

cond time into their mother's womb to be born!" Jesus answered, "Very truly I tell you, no one can enter the kingdom of God unless they are born of water and the Spirit. Flesh gives birth to flesh, but the Spirit gives birth to spirit (John 3:3-6).

Norm and I love to travel to other nations to pray. Intercession is one of the main strategies we use to remove the darkness and prepare the area for salvation. We stayed with our friends in southern Spain on several occasions. Their apartment was on the eighth floor with a balcony overlooking Gibraltar. I would love to walk out on the balcony, look below me at Spain, look in front of me at Gibraltar, and look far out in the distance and see Morocco. It was a perfect place to pray for all three nations. I knew in my heart that light was released as I partnered with the Holy Spirit in prayer.

It is pointless to try to evangelize a city or region without first bathing that area in intensive intercession. Here at IHOP, the mission's students going to the nations spend four hours a day in prayer on the field. It is definitely the strategic way to reach nations in the power of the Holy Spirit. He is our partner, and He is deeply involved in reaching the lost as we pray. He wants to take us deeper in partnership as we pray for the lost.

Could it be that our prayers are essential to gathering in the harvest? Our intercession may well cultivate the soil of the hearts of the lost to receive the gospel seed (Mark 4:8). They also may battle against the enemy as he comes to snatch away the seed (Mark 4:14-15). And they may help lift the darkness away from the eyes of unbelievers (Acts 26:17-18), so they can see the glorious light of the gospel (2 Corinthians 4:3-4). Nothing should motivate us to pray for the harvest more than the knowledge that multitudes may receive Christ because we prayed. What greater joy could there be than knowing that our prayers helped lift the darkness so the lost might see the Light? Someday we may find, indeed, that heaven is populated with multitudes of our answered prayers.[13] Dick Eastman

Deeper Still Life Application
How to Partner with the Holy Spirit
in Praying for the Lost

In this chapter we've learned about the Holy Spirit and prayer, the Holy Spirit's ministry and power, and praying for the lost. In this application we'll focus on how to partner with the Holy Spirit in praying for the lost.

As you begin, come before God in silent prayer. Expect the Holy Spirit to speak to you and help you to pray for the lost. Ask Him to bring the names of individuals to mind that do not know Christ personally. Wait on Him. Then take a piece of paper or your prayer journal, and write down those names. Begin to partner with the Holy Spirit and pray the following. You may want to pray this for your city as well. The Holy Spirit will guide and direct you as you pray. He will help you to pray on target prayers for each individual.

- Pray that He will soften the hearts of the unsaved - Many have hard hearts but the Holy Spirit is able to soften them through prayer.

  For he is our God and we are the people of his pasture, the flock under his care. Today, if you hear his voice, do not harden your hearts (Psalm 95:7-8a).

- Pray that the spiritual blindness will be removed - Satan has blinded the minds of the lost, but the Holy Spirit can lift that blindness.

  The god of this age has blinded the minds of unbelievers, so that they cannot see the light of the gospel that displays the glory of Christ, who is the image of God (2 Corinthians 4:4).

- Pray that their minds will understand truth - The Holy Spirit is able to open their eyes to see, removing the darkness and causing them to understand.

  They are darkened in their understanding and separated from the life of God because of the ignorance that is in them due to the hardening of their hearts (Ephesians 4:18).

- Pray that they will repent and turn to God - The Holy Spirit is able to bring men and women to repentance.

  Repent, then, and turn to God, so that your sins may be wiped out, that times of refreshing may come from the Lord (Acts 3:19).

- Pray for workers to be sent to the harvest field to reach the lost - The Holy Spirit is able to touch the hearts of workers, causing them to go into the harvest to share the good news of the gospel.

  Ask the Lord of the harvest, therefore, to send out workers into his harvest field (Matthew 9:38).

Pray for your list of individuals every day this week. Ask the Lord to help you to be a witness and light in their lives if the opportunity arises (Matthew 5:14-16).

How to Help Others Partner with the Holy Spirit in Praying for the Lost

Get together with an individual or group and spend time in God's presence, asking Him to bring to mind individuals who do not know Christ. Write down those names and share them with one another. Have a time of praying the requests in this life application for those on your list. Let the Holy Spirit guide you in your prayers. Be aware of His leading. Close with a time of thanksgiving for what He is doing in those lives.

Pray for everyone on that list each day this week. Expect the Holy Spirit to work. Pray that God helps each one of you to be a light in their lives.

My Prayer to God

Lord, I pray that You would teach me to yield myself to Your Spirit. Holy Spirit, teach me to trust You as a living person who leads my life and my prayers. Help me to understand Your ministry and power. Help me to understand You as my Comforter, Counselor, Helper, Advocate, Intercessor, and Strengthener. I long to see a demonstration of Your power in my life just as the Apostle Paul did (1 Corinthians 2:2-5). I thank you that You indwell, seal, sanctify, and empower me. You guide me, teach me, and pray through me. Help me to partner with You in everything I do. Transform my life completely with Your power. Make me sensitive to Your promptings, and teach me to partner with You in prayer in a deeper way.

I thank you that the darkness vanishes as I pray for the lost. Thank you for convicting the world of sin, righteousness, and judgment. I pray that you will soften the hearts of [Name those who do not know Christ]. Remove the spiritual blindness from their eyes, and help them to understand the truth about You. Bring them to repentance and salvation (Acts 3:19). Help me to be Your light in their lives. Help me to let my light shine before men, that they may see my good deeds and glorify my Father in heaven (Mathew 5:16). Show me how to be Your witness and how to show acts of love to them. I believe that You are working in their lives even as I pray. In Jesus' name, amen.

CHAPTER FOUR

DEEPER IN STRATEGIC PRAYER

Lord, let your ear be attentive to the prayer
of this your servant and to the prayer of your servants
who delight in revering your name.
Give your servant success today by granting
him favor in the presence of this man.
Nehemiah 1:11

NEHEMIAH BELIEVED IN PRAYER. He saw it as the key to his long-term strategy in accomplishing the mighty works of God. He committed himself to work until the job of building the walls of Jerusalem were completed. He viewed prayer not like a short-term sprinter, but more like a long distance runner winning the race through a strategic plan of endurance and faithfulness.

And God gave him success.

In Nehemiah 1, after hearing the sad report of the condition of Jerusalem, Nehemiah took the lead in seeing the walls rebuilt in the city. He integrated prayer successfully all throughout his building project, cultivating a continual dependence on God for direction and help.

Nehemiah's strategy was prayer.

When he first found out about the city, he mourned, fasted, and prayed (Nehemiah 1:5-11). He stopped his activities and gave himself fully to God in prayer. Then God gave him the desire and strategy to build the walls of Jerusalem (Nehemiah 2:12). Nehemiah responded in obedience to God's plan with an attitude of worship (Nehemiah 1:5). He persisted in prayer as he confessed his sin and the sins of the people (Nehemiah 1:6-7).

> *...let your ear be attentive and your eyes open to hear the prayer your servant is praying before you day and night for your servants, the people of Israel. I confess the sins we Israelites, including myself and my father's family, have committed against you. We have acted very wickedly toward you. We have not obeyed the commands, decrees and laws you gave your servant Moses* (Nehemiah 1:6-7).

Nehemiah remembered God's promises and strategically prayed God's Word back to Him (Nehemiah 1:8-9; Deuteronomy 30:2-4). His prayers were bold (Nehemiah 1:10-11) and specific (Nehemiah 1:11; 2:4-5). He knew that God wanted him to rebuild the city. Although he was fearful, because he prayed he took a step of action by asking the King for help (Nehemiah 2:1-9). He sought the wisdom of God and prayed as he answered the king's question, "What is it you want?"

The king granted Nehemiah's desires far beyond his request, and Nehemiah gave God the glory (Nehemiah 2:7-9). When opposition arose, Nehemiah became a mighty prayer warrior (Nehemiah 4:4-5). He called his people together and posted guards to protect the builders as they prayed (Nehemiah 4:9). Nehemiah understood the strategy of prayer for accomplishing God's work.

He was a man who prioritized prayer. The work started in prayer, continued in prayer, and was completed through prayer. God was honored and His Kingdom was advanced because this intercessor understood the strategy of prayer.

Perhaps you are wondering how you can be like Nehemiah who knew how to be prayerful right in the midst of warfare. Discover ways to touch heaven's strategy of prayer. Learn about the necessity and cost of prioritizing prayer. Find out how to find strategic joy in the midst of warfare. God wants to take us deeper in strategic prayer. Let's learn to be prayer warriors like Nehemiah!

Prayer is the Strategy of Heaven

Intercession is standing before the court of heaven and pleading a case or cause before a Holy awesome God. There are things that deeply touch the righteous Heart of the Father and above all, He is jealous of His glory...["[1]] Michael Howard, *Proven Arrows of Intercession*

Our God is a mighty warrior. He is a God who has a strategic plan. You and I can take part in this strategic plan.

I doubt if very many of us wake up in the morning and enter the day realizing that we are at war and that strategy is of utmost importance. The truth is that prayer is the greatest strategy in the world. Prayer is the strategy of heaven. As we use this mighty weapon, God then gives us His strategy for life on earth just like He did with Nehemiah.

The majority of the Church worldwide has not, yet, awakened to this strategic weapon of prayer and intercession. If we did we would be using it daily, and our prayer meetings would be packed to overflowing. I envision the day coming when we will begin to realize more and more that nothing happens without prayer.

Often in the natural we look to man-made methods and schemes to get the job done. We think big money and promotion will reach the world. We try harder with our human ingenuity. No. That will never work, at least not long-term. Prayer and intercession will prepare the way for the harvest. We must choose to use heaven's strategy rather than man's human devices. We must set our minds above and learn to intercede. Prayer is the strategy of heaven. We read in Colossians 3:1-2:

> *Since, then, you have been raised with Christ, set your hearts on things above, where Christ is, seated at the right hand of God. Set your minds on things above, not on earthly things.*

It is in prayer that God gives us heavenly strategy to do the work on earth that will touch the world. I have seen this over and over again. In intercession God gives us the greatest plan. In the quiet place God opens to us His greatest secrets. Everything that will make a difference has to have the touch of the supernatural. God does the work through us, and He gives us His plan in prayer. Multitudes of Christians use the strategy of prayer on the Global Day of Prayer. Corporate intercession takes place in over 220 nations. But it must continue with increasing intensity and commitment. The days we are living in are evil, and nothing but intense intercession will bring in the harvest.

A woman came to a missionary in India asking him to prevent a certain Christian from praying for her anymore. She was asked how she knew that Christian was praying for her. She replied, "I used to perform my worship to the idols quite easily before and now I can't. He told me he was praying for me and my family, and now my son and daughter have become Christians. If he continues to pray, I may become a Christian as well. Things happen when he prays. Somebody must make him stop!"

This Christian knew that prayer was the strategy of heaven and so did the idol worshipper who did not want to experience the power of prayer. God wants us to go deeper in strategic prayer. These are days of opportunity, and God is raising up intercessors to touch people's lives in every nation. Never underestimate the true potential of prayer. Ephesians 5:15-16 says:

> *Be very careful, then, how you live—not as unwise but as wise, making the most of every opportunity, because the days are evil.*

Never fail to realize that an hour in prayer can make a huge difference in the strategic outcome of your day and in the lives of others. But how do we touch this heavenly strategy?

Ways to Touch Heaven's Strategy of Prayer

I find in my personal life that a faster way to enter into the throne room of God is through worship, praying the Word of God, and fasting. This brings me quickly into heaven's perspective. These are three secrets to a deeper prayer life. We have every spiritual blessing in Christ. Ephesians 1:3-5 says:

> *Praise be to the God and Father of our Lord Jesus Christ, who has blessed us in the heavenly realms with every spiritual blessing in Christ. For he chose us in him before the creation of the world to be holy and blameless in his sight. In love he predestined us to be adopted as his sons through Jesus Christ...*

We touch heaven through our praise, through praying the Word, and when we deny ourselves through fasting. We are then able to concentrate more fully on God's heart. Let's look at these three ways with quotes by Michael Howard, a mighty intercessor, in his book called *Proven Arrows of Intercession:*

- **Worship and Praise.** Worship, praise, and thanksgiving should be incorporated into your life as much as possible. When you are down or discouraged, try the medicine of praise and thanksgiving. It is a good medicine because it puts your attention back upon the greatness and the glory of God. Praise is a powerful weapon of war.

  We can never underestimate praise as one of the greatest and most powerful weapons of war which the Lord has placed in our hands. And, when praise becomes high praise, it commands the unlimited resources of heaven because it gives absolute glory to the Lord. In a way which is beyond our understanding, deliverance and redemption are wrought through praise with great power for such conclusively speak of the supreme victory of Jesus.[2]

- **Pray the Word of God.** If you want to grow in your prayer life, start praying the Bible regularly. God loves us to pray His Word and use the S   word of the Spirit in intercession for the lost. It keeps us on-target, and we begin to think the very thoughts of God.

  The promises and blessings of God's Word are conditional. What God has done before, He will do again under the same climate and by the same standards. It is for this reason that intercession must be solidly built upon and directed by the Word. This means that the intercessor must know and quote the Word. This is not so the devil can hear but because a case must be made before the Lord... God is committed to His Word and the fulfilling of it.[3]

- **Fast and Pray.** Fasting is key to a powerful prayer life. Fasting together with prayer will help you to tap into heaven's riches and strategy in a way nothing else can. It quiets your outer man so that your inner man can hear the heartbeat of heaven. We'll look more thoroughly at the whole area of fasting in a later chapter.

Jesus was always "prayed and fasted up" while the disciples were not. This is why He always had authority in any situation. It is too late in the crisis to "get fasted and prayed up," so to speak... The benefits, blessings and powers of fasting are clearly revealed in the Word. Firstly, fasting brings the flesh into submission in all areas and herein lies the secret of the power... Fasting is a total denial of self that is mandatory if one is to be a true disciple of Jesus (Mt. 16:24). Thirdly, there is a mysterious relationship between fasting and the power of heaven intervening on our behalf.[4]

Is it always easy to go heaven's way? No, we are so often tempted by earth's attraction. We are tempted by quick results and man-made schemes, by things that look so good. We are attracted by fleshly fame and fortune. But in reality prayer is what really will get the job done.

Let's learn to prioritize it. Prayer and intercession will bring glory to the King and touch earth with heaven's riches. Prayer is the strategy of heaven. Prayer is the work, the strategic work, of the Kingdom. Prayer will prepare the way for the King.

Never forget this truth, because your enemy will tempt you in every way possible to get the job done through human resources. He will promise you a quick, painless way to get results. But, the quickest way is to go straight to the King in prayer. And He will reveal to you a strategy of life that will release His greatest glory through you here on earth. Why is this true? It is because you will be living and doing exactly what you were made for.

And I promise you that this is a joyful and fulfilling way to live.

God puts no limitations on His ability to save through true praying. No hopeless conditions, no accumulation of difficulties, no desperation in distance or circumstances can hinder the success of real prayer. The possibilities of prayer are linked to the infinite rectitude and to the omnipotent power of God. There is nothing too hard for God to do. God is pledged if we ask, we shall receive. God can withhold nothing from faith and prayer.[5]
E. M. Bounds, *E. M. Bounds on Prayer*

Prioritizing Prayer

To the average Christian the command "pray without ceasing" is simply a needless and impossible life of perfection. Who can do it? We can get to heaven without it. To the true believer, on the contrary, it holds out the promise of the highest happiness, of a life crowned by all the blessings that can be brought down on souls through his intercession. And as he perseveres, it becomes increasingly his highest aim upon earth, his highest joy, his highest experience of the wonderful fellowship with the holy God."[6]
Andrew Murray, *Andrew Murray on Prayer*

We always have enough time for the things we prioritize.

A key to the Christian's life is to prioritize prayer. Too many things in life are calling out for our attention. Therefore, we must learn to prioritize prayer. It is something we have to give our utmost attention to. The enemy is TOO clever, and he will try to steal our time. This is where he will resist us the most. We each need to have a vision for prayer. Vision determines priorities, and our priorities determine our destinies. Put prayer as a high priority in your life. When you do, you will go deeper in strategic prayer.

In Acts 12:5, we read about fervent prayer for Peter by the church. They prayed with intense earnestness. Peter was in trouble! The word "earnestness" in the Greek means "stretched-out-edly." Their souls were stretched out with intense earnestness towards God. It was like a runner using every nerve and muscle stretched out toward the goal.

Jesus also prayed with intense earnestness in Luke 22:44 so that even his sweat became as drops of blood. God desires that we learn to prioritize prayer and seek to be a man or woman of intense earnestness in prayer. The Bible speaks about devoting ourselves to prayer in Colossians 4:2. The Amplified Bible says:

> *Be earnest and unwearied and steadfast in your prayer [life], being [both] alert and intent in [your praying] with thanksgiving.*

Dorothy Haskins in her book, *A Prayer Guide to Prayer*, tells about an excellent concert violinist who was asked the secret of her mastery of the violin. She responded, "Planned neglect." She explained how so many things demanded her time. After breakfast, she would do her normal duties such as straightening her room, cleaning, and several other things that seemed necessary. She would then turn to her violin after finishing all her work. But she was unable to accomplish what she should on the violin. So she reversed the order, and neglected everything until her practice period on the violin was completed.

That was the secret to her success. She put her violin practice first.

How often we are like this violinist and put prayer at the end of what needs to be done. It can be last on our list. It must be first. It must be prioritized in our lives, if we want to have a life dedicated to God's glory. Prioritizing prayer is one of the secrets to a deeper prayer life. We need to prayer first now and not wait.

The world is getting worse with each passing day as crime and terrorism increase. With earthquakes killing thousands, hurricane predictions on the horizon, plus famines, hunger, homelessness, and needs everywhere—if ever there was a need for earnestness in our prayer meetings, it is now.

But you and I don't have to wait for an emergency situation in our city or nation. We already live in an emergency situation. God has sounded the alarm. Millions do not yet know Christ. Throughout history, there were praying individuals who knew the seriousness of the hour and prioritized prayer every day. Let's look at some of these examples from history.

Historical Examples

Christ, who in this as well as in other things is our example, spent many whole nights in prayer. His custom was to pray much. He had His habitual place to pray. Many long seasons of praying made up His history and character. Paul prayed day and night. Daniel's three daily prayers took time away from other important interests. David's morning, noon, and night praying was doubtless on many occasions very long and involved. While we have no specific account of the time these Bible saints spent in prayer, the indications are that they devoted much time to prayer, and on some occasions long seasons of praying were their custom.[8] E. M. Bounds, *E. M. Bounds on Prayer*

These prayer warriors prioritized prayer in their everyday life. Even though some of them had ill health, busy lives, or were very old, they still were able to put prayer first.

- **84-year old Anna.** She was very old but prayed and fasted night and day for years. See Luke 2:36.

- **David Brainerd.** He spent whole days in prayer as he cried out for the salvation of the Native Americans.

- **E. M. Bounds.** He was an eager and intense man of prayer who was able to soar into the heavens in his prayer life. He prayed such prayers of faith that believed God for the impossible. He also wrote many outstanding books on prayer.

- **John Hyde.** He was a missionary to India who paid a high price for prayer. He spent thirty days and nights in intercession and was ranked as a mad enthusiast in prayer.

We influence others as we, ourselves, spend time in prayer. Our short prayers are effective when we have prayed long ones. We must learn to prevail with God just as these men and women did. Jacob had victory because he wrestled all night with God. The Bible exhorts us to pray continually in 1 Thessalonians 5:16-18:

> *Be joyful always; pray continually; give thanks in all circumstances, for this is God's will for you in Christ Jesus.*

The Cost of Prioritizing Prayer

Devote yourselves to Prayer, being watchful and thankful.
Colossians 4:2

Those who pray receive a blessing for now and for eternity that far outweighs the cost. They learn the secret to a joyful and strategic life. But choosing to prioritize prayer has a price tag. It will cost us to put prayer at the top of our responsibilities, but it is well worth the effort. It will cost us:

- **Time.** We must devote ourselves to prayer. We may have to give up other good things in order to do the best.

- **Energy.** Prayer can be hard work and very intense physically. It will take concentrated energy to pray. God may call us to pray in the middle of the night. See Isaiah 64:7.

- **A Pure Motive.** Prayer is often done in secret. We need to have a pure motive when we pray. God will reward us openly. See Matthew 6:6.

- **Faith.** We don't often see results immediately when we pray, and this takes great faith. But God does answer prayer in a powerful way if we persevere in faith. See Hebrews 11:1, 6.

The full-time intercessory missionaries here at the International House of Prayer in Kansas City spend 24 hours a week in the prayer room. It demands their time, energy, and faith. The cost is high—but there is great joy in the prayer room.

Let's rise to a new level in prioritizing prayer and intercession. May God help us to keep it at the center of our life even through the busy days. This is a strategic way to order our lives. May He give us the grace to prioritize prayer, not only when emergency situations arise in our own personal lives, but also as we live in the emergency situation we all face in the end times.

I pray that God will encourage your heart to count the cost and say, "Yes" to the ministry of intercession. May you be one to influence others to choose to prioritize prayer in their life. Through prayer, you can have joy right in the midst of the battle. May the following quote be true in our life in a day when intercession is rapidly increasing throughout the world.

> They may start from different points, and travel by different roads, but they converge to one point: they are one in prayer. To them, God is the center of attraction, and prayer is the path that leads to God. These men (and women) do not pray occasionally—not a little or at odd times. But they pray in such a way that their prayers enter into and shape their very characters. They pray so as to affect their own lives and the lives of others, and to cause the history of the church to influence the current of the times. They spend much time in prayer, not because they watch the shadow of the dial or the hands on the clock, but be-

cause it is to them so momentous and engaging a business that they can scarcely quit.[9] E. M. Bounds, *E. M. Bounds on Prayer*

Strategic Joy
in the Midst of Warfare

Joy and gladness are the currency on which heaven runs... Joy is deep-rooted happiness in the presence, person and nature of God. It sits in our heart and directs our life, displacing grief, mourning and sadness. When we have a quiet, God-given joy bubbling up inside us, the negative is pushed out.[10] Graham Cooke, *Drawing Close*

Living strategically in the end times is a key to victory. The strategy of the enemy is to steal your joy. God's strategy is that we are joyful in the midst of spiritual warfare. This may seem quite difficult when facing hard, strenuous battles.

In 2006, I was going through some difficult warfare. Praying towards and pressing through in battle to get several books on prayer published, and a new Intercessors Arise International website up and running, was not an easy task. Anything to do with writing about prayer faced the greatest spiritual attacks. I knew this. The enemy tried to bring discouragement into my life. Along with this was the battle that year with my health.

But there was another way of looking at all of these problems. We have the hope and reality of heaven. It is time we bring the joy of heaven to earth. All of heaven loves to rejoice!

Joy is our strategy against the works of the devil.

In this trial God began to speak strongly to my heart. He was saying, "Do not despair or give up." At that point, I realized that the enemy wanted to invade my life with a spirit of discouragement and despair, but God wanted to give me joy instead. Doesn't that sound like a better alternative? I thought so and began to study about joy. I studied verse after verse about joy.

Did you know that there are nearly three hundred verses in the Bible about joy?

The Bible commands us to be joyful always and pray continually (1 Thessalonians 5:16), to be joyful in God (Hebrews 3:18), to consider it pure joy when we encounter trials (James 1:2), to tell of God's works with songs of joy (Psalm 107:22), and the list goes on and on. Joy is a fruit of the Spirit (Galatians 5:22); there is joy in God's presence (Acts 2:28), and the Holy Spirit gives joy (Luke 10:21). God wants to anoint us with the oil of joy (Hebrews 1:9), and He wants us to pray with joy (Philippians 1:4). Throughout Scripture, we are exhorted to shout and sing for joy (Psalm 118:15; Isaiah 52:9). Even the heavens, the earth, the mountains, and the trees are commanded to sing for joy!

We are called to a high quality of life that includes joy in the midst of difficult circumstances. Graham Cooke says the following about joy:

> We are called to this same thriving quality of life, that no matter our circumstances, we live in the promise of God's joy. It is impossible to keep God from being happy, and because of that, His Church cannot be denied joy either. Sadness and grief can only overlay our joy; it cannot prevent a breakthrough into it. We may have to look hard on days for that cheerfulness, but it is always present in the heart of God. Sadness must be infiltrated by joy.[11]

Why then do we sometimes get heavy-hearted?

It is because we are in spiritual warfare, and Satan hates prayer so strongly. He doesn't mind when we do many other things, but he trembles when we pray. He actually attacks us with a spirit of despair or discouragement. He will do everything he can to stop the advance of the prayer movement.

At times when a heavy weight of discouragement threatens to overwhelm you, and if there is no known sin in your life, you can be sure that the enemy is attacking you with a spirit of despair or discouragement. I prayed against this in my own life and a remarkable thing happened. The heaviness lifted.

I pray that you know the joy of the Lord as your strength and that every trace of discouragement or despair is lifted from your life. If you need hope, I pray that the stronghold of hopelessness will be broken in the name of Jesus. I pray that the joy of the Lord will permeate your prayer life and everything that you do.

God does not want you to be disheartened, but He longs to fill you with His joy. He has anointed you to help others who are going through difficulty and to actually bestow the oil of gladness, joy, and praise on those who have a spirit of despair. This is the job description of Jesus. We are to be like Him with this job description as well. We read in Isaiah 61:1-3:

> *The Spirit of the Sovereign Lord is on me, because the Lord has anointed me to proclaim good news to the poor. He has sent me to bind up the brokenhearted, to proclaim freedom for the captives and release from darkness for the prisoners, to proclaim the year of the Lord's favor and the day of vengeance of our God, to comfort all who mourn, and provide for those who grieve in Zion—to bestow on them a crown of beauty instead of ashes, the oil of joy instead of mourning, and a garment of praise instead of a spirit of despair. They will be called oaks of righteousness, a planting of the Lord for the display of his splendor.*

I remember when tropical storm Ernesto passed through our city. Rain was pouring down, the streets were flooded, and clouds and wind were everywhere. People were told to stay in their homes due to the flooding. It was hard to imagine sunshine in the midst of the storm.

Recently on a flight, our plane was flying through many clouds on the right and the left as it was ascending. It was scary. Suddenly the plane came out into the sunshine above all the threatening clouds.

Circumstances can be like both of these examples. Heaviness and darkness can invade our lives because of what is happening around us. When we can't see past the clouds and trials, the devil takes the opportunity to attack us with discouragement or despair. This is when we must rise above the clouds, and see life from God's perspective and vantage point through His Word. The sunshine will one day return—we do not have to live in gloom or despair—God has provided a way out.

If you are feeling down and can't seem to get out of it, take the authority in prayer that is rightfully yours, and break that discouragement using the name of Jesus. His name is powerful.

Then ask God to fill you with His joy and peace. Write down the positive things in your life, and thank God for each one of them. God is able to push the negatives out as you begin to praise Him and dwell on the positive things He has provided for you. Don't live your life according to your earthly circumstances but according to your position in Christ. Remember that you:

- Are the temple of God (1 Corinthians 3:16).

- Are a new creation (2 Corinthians 5:17).

- Are seated in heavenly places (Ephesians 1:3-6).

- Are chosen of God (Ephesians 1:11).

- Are God's possession (Ephesians 1:14).

- Are able to do all things through Christ (Philippians 4:13).

- Are complete in Him (Colossians 2:9-10).

- Are a royal priesthood (1 Peter 2:9).

- Are a kingdom of priests (Revelation 1:6).

Strategic joy in the midst of warfare is yours. God wants to bring you deeper in strategic, joyful prayer. It's one of the secrets to a deeper prayer life.

This is how you will live victoriously. This is your birthright!

> Don't deny yourself that which is your birthright as a child of God. Don't be satisfied with a joyless life. There ought to be in every Christian a deep, settled fullness of the joy of Christ that no circumstance of life can dispel. This comes as you allow the Holy Spirit to express Himself in your life. One of the fruits of the Spirit is joy (Gal. 5:22). This joy is unlike any happiness that is produced by the world. It fills you and permeates everything you do. Jesus did not pray that you would merely be happy or even that you would escape grief. He prayed that you would have the same joy that the Father had given Him: a divine joy, a joy that comes from a deep and unwavering relationship with the Fa-

ther. It is a joy that is grounded so firmly in a relationship with God that no change in circumstances could ever shake it. This is the kind of joy that Christ is praying will be in you.[12] Henry and Richard Blackaby, *Experiencing God Day-by-Day*

Deeper Still Life Application
How to Have a Strategic Prayer Life

We've looked at how prayer is the strategy of heaven. We saw our need to prioritize prayer and how we can have strategic joy right in the midst of warfare. I find in my life personally that a quicker way to enter into the throne room of God is through worship, praying the Word of God, and choosing to rejoice. This brings us into heaven's perspective. With notebook and pen in hand, quiet yourself before God, and do the following:

- **Worship and praise God** - Have a time of worship, praise, and thanksgiving. Make a list of everything you are thankful for, including the difficult things. When you are down or discouraged, try the medicine of praise and thanksgiving. It is a good medicine, because it puts our attention back upon the greatness and the glory of God.

- **Pray the Word of God** - Key Biblical prayers are the apostolic prayers of Paul: Romans 3:1-5; 10:1; 15:5-7, 13; Ephesians 1:17-19; 3:16-19; Phil. 1:9-11; 4:2-4; Colossians 1:9-12; 1 Thessalonians 5:23-24; and 2 Thessalonians 1:11-12.

  Begin praying these prayers to God in your devotional times along with your personal prayers, worship, and praise. God loves us to pray His Word every day. It keeps us on-target, and we begin to think the very thoughts of God.

- **Choose to rejoice** - The Bible commands us to be joyful always in 1 Thessalonians 5:16. Meditate on the following Scriptures about living a joyful life and write a prayer of joy to God, thanking Him for your present circumstances, good or bad. Meditate on Isaiah 52:9; Psalm 107:22; 118:15; Luke 10:21; Acts 2:28; Galatians 5:22; Philippians 1:4; Hebrews 2:9; 3:18; and James 1:2.

Practice extravagant worship and praise using the Word of God every day this week. Make a personal thanksgiving list, and pray the apostolic prayers daily in your quiet time. These are big secrets to a deeper prayer life. Pray "My Prayer to God" several times as well.

How to Help Others
Have a Strategic Prayer Life

Get together with an individual or group, and read through the apostolic prayers of Paul. You may want to have them printed out beforehand. I have included them on the following pages. The capitalized words are helpful isolated phrases to use in prayer as well as in song.

Start with a time of worship and praise using a Psalm of your choice. Then begin to pray the Word of God using the apostolic prayers of Paul. You will discover that this leads into a very strategic prayer time. End your meeting by praying "My Prayer to God." It would be helpful to meet together a few more times for a discussion of this chapter, personal encouragement, fasting together, and strategic prayer times.

My Prayer to God

Lord, I thank You that prayer is the strategy of heaven. Enable me to live wisely, making the most of every opportunity in prayer (Ephesians 5:15-16). Teach me how to pray Your Word daily. Help me to incorporate fasting into my life on a regular basis. I want my inner man to know Your heart. I want to tap into heaven's riches in a deeper way. Help me to prioritize prayer with my time and my energy. Purify my motives and develop my faith to believe You for greater things. Help me to grow in praise and thanksgiving, especially during the hard times. I want to know strategic joy right in the midst of the battles that I face.

Thank You that Your divine joy goes beyond my circumstances. Thank You that I can know You and follow Your plans every day of my life. Help me to set my heart on things above and exercise the strategy of prayer more in my life (Colossians 3:1-2). I pray that Your love may abound in my life in knowledge and discernment and that I may approve the things that are excellent, that I may be sincere and without offense, being filled with the fruits of righteousness in You to the glory and praise of God (Philippians 1:9-11). Bring me deeper in strategic prayer for Your glory. I will sacrifice thank offerings and tell of Your works with songs of joy (Psalm 107:21-22). I praise Your name. You have been so good to me. In Jesus' name, amen.

The New Testament Apostolic Prayers of Paul

Prayer for revelation of Jesus' beauty and the Bride's destiny unto transforming our heart.

"… the Father of glory, may give to you the SPIRIT OF WISDOM AND REVELATION IN THE KNOWLEDGE OF HIM, the eyes of your understanding being enlightened; that you may know what is the HOPE OF HIS CALLING, what are the riches of the GLORY OF HIS INHERITANCE IN THE SAINTS, and what is the exceeding GREATNESS OF HIS POWER TOWARD US" (Ephesians 1:17-19).

Prayer for the release of supernatural strength in the heart unto experiencing God's emotions.

"… that He would grant you, according to the riches of His glory, TO BE STRENGTHENED WITH MIGHT THROUGH HIS SPIRIT IN THE INNER MAN, that Christ may dwell in your hearts through faith; that you, being rooted and grounded in love, MAY BE ABLE TO COMPREHEND with all the saints what is the width and length and depth and height—to know the love of Christ which passes knowledge; that you may be filled with all the fullness of God" (Ephesians 3:16-19).

Prayer for God's love to abound in our heart resulting in discernment and righteousness.

"And this I pray, that YOUR LOVE MAY ABOUND still more and more in knowledge and all discernment, that you may APPROVE THE THINGS THAT ARE EXCELLENT, that you may be sincere and without offense till the day of Christ, being FILLED WITH THE FRUITS OF RIGHTEOUSNESS which are by Jesus Christ, to the glory and praise of God" (Philippians 1:9-11).

Prayer to know God's will, to be fruitful in ministry and strengthened by intimacy with God.

"We… do not cease to pray for you, and to ask that you may be filled with the KNOWLEDGE OF HIS WILL in all wisdom and spiritual understanding; that you may have a WALK WORTHY OF THE LORD, fully pleasing Him, BEING FRUITFUL in every good work and increasing in the knowledge of God; STRENGTHENED WITH ALL MIGHT, according to His glorious power, for all patience and longsuffering with joy; giving thanks to the Father who has qualified us to be partakers of the inheritance of the saints in the light" (Colossians 1:9-12).

Prayer for unity in the Church across a city or region.

"Now may the God of patience and comfort GRANT YOU TO BE LIKE-MINDED toward one another, according to Christ Jesus, THAT YOU MAY WITH ONE MIND AND ONE MOUTH glorify the God and Father of our Lord Jesus" (Romans 15:5-7).

Prayer to be filled with supernatural joy, peace and hope.

"Now may the God of hope FILL YOU WITH ALL JOY AND PEACE IN BELIEVING, THAT YOU MAY ABOUND IN HOPE by the power of the Holy Spirit" (Romans 15:13).

Prayer for Israel to be saved through Jesus.

"Brethren, my heart's desire and prayer to God for ISRAEL is that they may be saved" (Romans 10:1).

Prayer for the release of apostolic ministry and to abound in love and holiness.

"We rejoice for your sake before our God, night and day praying exceedingly that we may see your face and perfect what is lacking in your faith. Now may our God and Father Himself, and our Lord Jesus Christ, direct our way to you. And may the Lord make you increase and ABOUND IN LOVE to one another and to all... so that He may ESTABLISH YOUR HEARTS BLAMELESS IN HOLINESS before our God and Father at the coming of our Lord Jesus Christ with all His saints" (1 Thessalonians 3:9-13).

Prayer for the release of the Holy Spirit's power unto mature holiness.

"Now may the God of peace Himself sanctify you completely; and may your whole spirit, soul, and body be preserved blameless at the coming of our Lord Jesus Christ. He who calls you is faithful, who also will do it" (1 Thessalonians 5:23-24).

Prayer to be equipped and prepared to receive the fullness of God's destiny for the Church.

"Therefore we also pray always for you THAT OUR GOD WOULD COUNT YOU WORTHY OF THIS CALLING, AND FULFILL ALL THE GOOD PLEA-SURE OF HIS GOODNESS AND THE WORK OF FAITH WITH POWER, that the name of our Lord Jesus Christ may be glorified in you, and you in Him, according to the grace of our God and the Lord Jesus Christ" (2 Thessalonians 1:11-12).

Prayer for the Word to increase by the release of God's power to win unbelievers to Jesus.

"Finally, brethren, pray for us, THAT THE WORD OF THE LORD MAY RUN SWIFTLY AND BE GLORIFIED, just as it is with you, and that we may be delivered from unreasonable and wicked men; for not all have faith. But the Lord is faithful, who will establish you and guard you from the evil one. And we have confidence in the Lord concerning you, both that you do and will do the things we command you. NOW MAY THE LORD DIRECT YOUR HEARTS INTO THE LOVE OF GOD AND INTO THE PATIENCE OF CHRIST" (2 Thessalonians 3:1-5).

Prayer that God would open a door of evangelism through releasing His power on the Word.

"Continue earnestly in prayer, being vigilant in it with thanksgiving; meanwhile praying also for us, THAT GOD WOULD OPEN TO US A DOOR FOR THE WORD, to speak the mystery of Christ, for which I am also in chains, that I may make it manifest, as I ought to speak" (Colossians 4:2-4).

Prayer to be enriched with the supernatural gifts of the Holy Spirit leading unto righteousness.

"I thank my God always concerning you for the grace of God which was given to you by Christ Jesus, THAT YOU WERE ENRICHED IN EVERYTHING by Him in all utterance and all knowledge, even as the testimony of Christ was confirmed in you, so THAT YOU COME SHORT IN NO GIFT, eagerly waiting for the revelation of our Lord Jesus Christ, who will also confirm you to the end, THAT YOU MAY BE BLAMELESS in the day of our Lord Jesus Christ" (1 Corinthians 1:4-8).

༄༅

CHAPTER FIVE

DEEPER IN SPIRITUAL INSIGHT

*My son, if you accept my words
and store up my commands within you,
turning your ear to wisdom
and applying your heart to understanding...
then you will understand the fear of the LORD
and find the knowledge of God.
For the LORD gives wisdom; from his mouth
comes knowledge and understanding.*
Proverbs 2:1-2, 5-6

༄༅

WE KNEW OUR PRAYERS would make a difference. We were aware that this prayer journey was important. We were a large group gathered together with a single purpose—to glorify God in southern Spain through strategic, insightful prayers.

On this carefully planned journey, we called upon God for insight and understanding. We searched for wisdom as for hidden treasure.

There were several Messianic leaders and others from various countries that gathered for this purpose. It was a prayer journey aimed at seeking reconciliation and forgiveness through prayer. God gave us daily insight as we prayed together in various cities—Cordoba, Granada, Jerez, and others. We needed to actually be praying in those very locations to receive the spiritual insight that the Holy Spirit wanted to reveal.

Praying on-site is insightful praying which helps us to identify with our surroundings. God led us into identificational repentance over sins that occurred in those places hundreds of years earlier. One Messianic leader's wife was weeping intensely as she represented the Jewish wives who had lost their children centuries before. At another point while traveling from one city to another, God gave great insight unexpectedly right on the bus as the group was praying. As we prayer walked, God was giving insight to see below the surface, to discern the truth that was not immediately apparent.

I believe that this reconciliation prayer journey brought a degree of breakthrough in Spain. It was another step in bringing the glory of God into that land. God gave us a spirit of wisdom and revelation that not only affected our lives, but what God wanted to do in Spain.

God wants to take each of us deeper in spiritual insight. You may be asking, "But how can I learn to pray with insight? How can I gain discernment and wisdom just as this group did in Spain on that prayer journey?" Let's discover ways to pray that will enhance our insight. Let's learn how to write a crafted prayer and how to enthrone God through prayer mapping.

Praying with Insight

What does "praying with insight" mean? It means praying from the perspective of knowledge or understanding regarding the circumstances of the person or situation you are praying for. Insight is the power to see below the surface of a situation, to discern the inner nature or truth of something that is not immediately apparent. Although asking questions and doing research often sheds light on a situation, true insight is essentially a spiritual quality. As such it has its source in God: "I have more insight than all my teachers, for Thy testimonies are my meditation" (Psalm 119:99)[1] Jim Goll, *Father Forgive Us*

It is a wonderful thing to know that when we pray, God gives us insight into our situation. We do not beat around in the dark or pray non-relevant, empty prayers, but we can be assured that God will give us wisdom in our prayers if we ask for it. Our prayers can be potent with the insight of God and with a razor-sharp, Holy Spirit-inspired ability to see into the spiritual realm for how to best pray in a given situation. Intercessors should be the wisest people on earth because they are coming to the God of all wisdom with their requests. Proverbs 2:6 says:

> *For the LORD gives wisdom; from his mouth comes knowledge and understanding.*

God will lead and direct our intercession if we choose to ask Him to give us insight and wisdom. Gaining wisdom for intercession is more precious than rubies. We read in Proverbs 8:10-11:

> *Choose my instruction instead of silver, knowledge rather than choice gold, for wisdom is more precious than rubies, and nothing you desire can compare with her.*

Ask the Holy Spirit to direct you every time you begin a time of prayer. He will help you to see below the surface of a situation and discern the truth. Many times I have prayed prayers spontaneously that I later realized were prayers that were initiated by the Holy Spirit with His insight and wisdom that was far beyond my own understanding. I believe that God gives true spiritual insight, but we need to give Him time in order to obtain the type of insight that is beyond our comprehension and that is supernatural.

All of us can grow in this area. We need this for the end-times prayer movement. Our God is wiser than all enemy attacks, and He knows the end from the beginning. We are going to need God's insight as to how to pray as judgments increasingly come upon the earth.

God wants to give us quickness in intellect, a readiness in apprehension, and dexterity in action—He longs that we are able to judge what is most proper and useful in every prayer situation—He wants us to be wise and insightful in our prayers. We need to be ones who cry out for insight and discernment on a regular basis. Just this morning, I was crying out to God with all my heart to give me wisdom and insight.

The Power of Asking for Insight and Discernment

Similar to insight in source and meaning is discernment, the ability to comprehend that which is obscure, to distinguish or discriminate (in the positive sense) between good and evil, true and false, right and wrong, especially where (on the surface at least) the differences are very subtle. "And this I pray, that your love may abound still more and more in real knowledge and all discernment, so that you may approve the things that are excellent..." (Philippines 1:9-10)[2] Jim Goll, *Father Forgive Us*

There is power in seeking God for insight, wisdom, and discernment. God wants us to be sharp-sighted with the ability to perceive the difference between right and wrong. Webster's Dictionary says that the word "insight" means: "sight or view of the interior of anything; deep inspection or view, thorough knowledge or skill."[3] God wants to make us into skillful prayer warriors with the ability to see into the inner depths the things that we are praying for. He wants to give us a deep view and understanding of how to pray. He wants us to approve of that which is excellent and pray accordingly.

Wisdom is: "Properly having knowledge, having the power of discerning and judging correctly, or of discriminating between what is true and what is false, between what is fit and proper, and what is improper." As God's people, we want to be wise in action and practice. God was pleased with Solomon's request Notice the power of asking for wisdom and insight.:

- **Solomon asked God for a discerning heart.**

    So give your servant a discerning heart to govern your people and to distinguish between right and wrong. For who is able to govern this great people of yours?" The Lord was pleased that Solomon asked for this (1 Kings 3:9-10).

- **Solomon was given a wise heart.**

    So God said to him, "Since you have asked for this and not for long life or wealth for yourself, nor have asked for the death of your enemies but for discernment in administering justice, I will do what you have asked. I will give you a wise and discerning heart, so that there will never have been anyone like you, nor will there ever be (1 Kings 3:12).

- **We learn the fear of the Lord.**

    The fear of the Lord is the beginning of knowledge, but fools despise wisdom and instruction (Proverbs 1:7).

- **Wisdom will be generously given.**

  If any of you lacks wisdom, he should ask God, who gives generously to all without finding fault, and it will be given to you. But when you ask, you must believe and not doubt... (James 1:5-6a).

- **God reveals His secret counsel.**

  Surely the Sovereign LORD does nothing without revealing his plans to his servants the prophets (Amos 3:7).

There are various ways that we can pray that will enhance our ability for insight and wisdom. You may have been involved in some of these ways yourself. Prayerwalking as we did in Spain has helped me to pray with wisdom and insight. It helps me to know how to pray as I see the situation before me where I walk and pray. I have done this numerous times in my own neighborhood. It is a tremendous way to pray with insight because you see the needs around you with your eyes. Prayerwalking is praying on site with insight.

Prayer watches are extended times of prayer that enables us to tap into the heart of God as we are waiting, watching, and praying for several hours. God is able to give us great insight because we are giving Him undistracted time. Micah 7:7 says:

> *But as for me, I watch in hope for the LORD, I wait for God my Savior; my God will hear me.*

Prayer and fasting is also very beneficial in receiving wisdom, insight, and divine revelation from God. It helps us to walk in humility, breaks our selfish ambition and pride, helps us to see God's priorities, and makes us more sensitive to the Holy Spirit. Praying over a map also gives us insight.

Get involved in all of these ways of praying because they will help enhance wisdom, discernment, and understanding in your life. Some key verses are: Psalm 59:9; 119:125; Proverbs 3:21; 10:13; 14:33; 16:21; and 17:24a. We read in Proverbs 4:7-8:

> *The beginning of wisdom is this: Get wisdom. Though it cost all you have, get understanding. Cherish her and she will exalt you; embrace her, and she will honor you.*

Sometimes we just do not know how to pray. Colossians 2:2-3 says: *My goal is that they may be encouraged in heart and united in love, so that they may have the full riches of complete understanding, in order that they may know the mystery of God, namely, Christ, in whom are hidden all the treasures of wisdom and knowledge.* All the treasures of wisdom and knowledge are hidden in Christ. Therefore, He will give us His wisdom as we pray and ask for it. He is our teacher. Psalm 51:6 says:

> *Yet you desired faithfulness even in the womb; you taught me wisdom in that secret place.*

My prayer for you is that God will give you a spirit of wisdom and revelation in your prayers. I pray that He will guide you supernaturally in your prayer life and that you will be an example of insight, discernment, and wisdom to others. I pray that your prayers will be powerful because they are prayers filled with Godly insight that sees below the surface, that you will be discerning and will keep wisdom in view (Proverbs 17:24a). I pray that your heart may be enlightened with hope and power to believe and that you will go deeper in spiritual insight than you have ever been before.

> God has called us to be a people of prayer and our churches to be houses of prayer. He has invited us to join Him in His redemptive plan for the world. God gives insight because whenever He gets ready to move, He reveals His plans to those who are seeking Him.[4] Jim Goll, *Father Forgive Us*

Enthroning God
Through Prayer Mapping

> The social and political climate of the world today calls for a massive mobilization of intercessors with a strategic battle plan for focused prayer. It seems that God is speaking to the church in an urgent manner in this very regard.[5] Dick Eastman, "Prayer Siege"

The battle in the nations is raging between the powers of light and the powers of darkness. In reaching our cities and nations through prayer and intercession, we are dethroning Satan and enthroning God. As we learn to pray with insight, we are enforcing the victory of God by transferring the seat of power and authority from the enemy and enthroning God through strategic prayer. Is it any wonder that we run in to such heavy spiritual battles? We are laying siege to the enemy through prayer. We are actually enthroning the King of kings through our intercession. We read in Psalm 113:4-6:

> *The LORD is exalted over all the nations, his glory above the heavens. Who is like the LORD our God, the One who sits enthroned on high, who stoops down to look on the heavens and the earth?*

A strategic way to enthrone God in a city is through praying over a map of that area.

I have often used maps to pray over nations, and I encourage you to do the same. Maps can help us to stay focused and faithful in prayer. In Spain, we had a big map of southern Spain (Andalucia) on the wall. I would often go to that map, lay my hands on it, and pray for that area of the world. I found that it would help me to pray with more fervency and with a focused vision for Spain. Prayer mapping will bring you deeper in spiritual insight.

The ship *Doulos* that I lived on for several years—that brought hope to nations all around the world—was started through prayer. The founder of Operation Mobilization, George Verwer, and others were praying numerous times over a map of the world. A God-idea came to him and the others one day while praying over the map. Water touches many cities in the world. Why not pray for a ship to bring the gospel to those cities? They began to pray fervently for God to provide a ship to reach the nations of the world that were surrounded by water.

God provided not one, but two ocean-going ships to bring hope to the nations. These men and women were enthroning God through praying over a map. Little did they realize the strategic plan that God was giving them at that time to literally touch millions with the gospel. Many, including myself, have been deeply impacted by this ministry.

Praying over a map can bring insight into our prayers as we see with our eyes the cities and nations we are praying for. Praying over a map was used in the Bible. God commissioned Ezekiel to lay siege to Jerusalem by using a prayer map. Ezekiel actually drew the city of Jerusalem on a piece of clay and laid it in front of himself to prayer. We read in Ezekiel 4:1-2: *Now, son of man, take a block of clay, put it in front of you and draw the city of Jerusalem on it. Then lay siege to it: Erect siege works against it, build a ramp up to it, set up camps against it and put battering rams around it.*

It is not a new thing; It is Biblical. Dick Eastman in his article "Prayer Siege" defines the word "siege" like this:

> Siege means "the act or process of surrounding and attacking a fortified place in such a way as to isolate it for the purpose of lessening the resistance of the defender and thereby making capture possible." Another definition reads, "any prolonged or persistent effort to overcome resistance." A third, more ancient definition is "seat of rule." So to lay siege in prayer would suggest a strategy that involves interceding for our neighbors or the nations to lessen their resistance to the Gospel.[6]

When God told Ezekiel to lay siege to Jerusalem, it was a powerful command. It is a strategic way to intercede for the city. It is a way to lessen the resistance of enemy forces. It is a way to enthrone God in the city. Because darkness and evil inhabit our cities, we must visually lay siege to them in prayer.

Getting a map of your city or nation can help you to lay siege to it in prayer. You are breaking down the resistance to the gospel as you surround the city with your prayers. Praying over a map can help you to break down the powers of darkness that are holding people in captivity.

Praying Over Your Map

> Fighting from her knees in many parts of the world, Christ's bride is already beginning to push back the forces of darkness for periods of time, during which millions are having the opportunity to hear the gospel for the first time and to be saved. We are literally living in the day of Psalm 2:8—we are asking the Father for the nations and they are coming to Him![7] Eddie and Alice Smith, *Drawing Closer to God's Heart*

In praying for your neighborhood, you may want to draw a map of the houses and families you are praying for. Define your mission field. Are you praying for a street, block, apartment complex, group of households, or a rural section? Map households in your community by making a homemade map or a simple list of persons in your neighborhood. Then begin to pray for guidance as you pray over your map. You may want to prayerwalk your neighborhood. You may also want to get a map of your city and begin praying over your city map.

All of this will help you to visually lay siege to your neighborhood or city, breaking dramatically the resistance of the enemy in your area. God will begin to work as you visually pray in this manner. He will give you strategic insight as to how to pray.

Purchase a world prayer map, and begin praying for the nations. This is a helpful tool for intercessors who like to pray daily over a map of the world. I have often used a map in my prayers. I find it to be motivational and practical. I like to see the nations I am praying for and know where they are located. I feel I am making a big difference in reaching the world through my prayers when I can visualize the nations. Try praying over a map. You will find this to be a powerful tool in prayer. This is one of the secrets to a deeper prayer life.

> The beauty of praying over a map of the world (as well as a hand-drawn map of our neighborhoods) is that it helps us contend for the lost in a far more specific manner. We're targeting actual nations and very real neighbors. This is far more meaningful than shallow prayers like "God bless all the people of the world, everywhere!"[8] Dick Eastman, "Prayer Siege"

Crafted Prayer

> "What is effective prayer? Very simply, it is a prayer God gives us permission to pray, prayed fervently, full of passion and power... Crafted prayer is about intention, aligning our request to God's will. There are prayers we need to write about our circumstances. There are prayers we need to write about our family and friends."[9] Graham Cooke, *Crafted Prayer*

Do you know how God wants you to pray in a given situation? Do you want to know how you can learn to pray with greater boldness and assurance over your circumstances? I know that I personally want to learn how to pray prayers that are crafted in heaven. I want to learn to pray God's will over my circumstances. Learning how to pray crafted prayers can help you to not only pray effectively, but to pray with great faith because you know deep in your heart that you are praying prayers that are initiated in heaven.

Crafted prayers can be written for your family members, your ministry, your church, your city, or nation. This does not hinder spontaneous prayer in any way, but actually releases it. Crafted prayer is purposeful and intentional. We carefully write down the revelation that God has given us as we wait and listen to Him. In moments of discouragement or when our heart is weak, we can take out our crafted prayer that has been well prepared and thought out in the past, and pray those prayers back to God over and over.

The Bible is filled with crafted prayers—Mathew 6:9-15; John 17; Romans 12:14-21; Ephesians 1:15-23; 3:14-19; and 1 Timothy 2:1-2. These are good prayers for all of us to pray.

I heard well-known author and speaker, Graham Cooke tell the story about how he wrote a carefully prepared, crafted prayer for his daughter before she went away to college. During that year she went through a very difficult time. Her father faithfully prayed his crafted prayer for his daughter, never giving up, and always knowing exactly how God wanted him to pray.

She grew spiritually through that year and in returning home, she told her father all of the things that God had done in her life. Her father took out his crafted prayer and showed it to his daughter. I'm sure he must have been smiling. God had answered that prayer exactly as he had prayed. His prayer was right on target, because he had taken the time to be still, listen, and then pray heaven's prayer over his daughter. In his book he says:

> When we know God's will, we enter into a certainty of the outcome. The confidence of the Holy Spirit fills us, and we become God's voice in a specific situation. Wonderfully, we are not praying to get an answer—we are praying with the answer. Because we know what God wants to do, we are free to follow the process God has ordained for us in the circumstances He has al-

lowed. It is time to use prayer as a weapon. We must grow up in our intercession, becoming the joyful, confident men and women God has destined us to be.[10]

I have a journal of prayer requests and prayers that I pray over and over. In this journal I pray for intercessors and the prayer movement as well as many other things. At times I go and pray these prayers regarding intercessors and prayer, and at other times I pray spontaneously in an entirely different way. It has helped me to think through exactly what I want to pray and how I want to pray about it. I wrote a crafted prayer regarding Intercessors Arise International that I am presently continuing to expand. I prayed, thought a lot about it, wrote down ideas and thoughts, and then crafted the prayer from what God had shown me.

A crafted prayer can be a real source of encouragement as we pray again and again over something that is close to our heart. I encourage you to get a journal and fill it with crafted prayers. During moments of deep darkness, this will be a source of incredible blessing because you are aligning your request with God's will. Crafted prayers will bring you *deeper still* in spiritual insight for those things that are closest to your heart.

I have included a crafted prayer at the end of each chapter in this book. These prayers cover the main thoughts from each chapter. You can pray them again and again in your personal life for yourself and others. Over time watch how God answers those prayers!

Learning to write a crafted prayer can be one of your greatest tools. It can help you to pray heaven's strategy in your situations here on earth. It can help you to declare God's will over your circumstances with great boldness, and it can help you pray specific, on-target prayers for your family members or church. You can do this with others as a family or a small group where you seek God's will and His answers together in prayer. Together you can pray over what God wants to do in your situation.

God loves us to pray His will over our circumstances—He loves to show us His heart—He is exceedingly glad when our faith rises up to the point where we declare His will over our situations in life with great boldness and confidence.

Crafted prayer is a wonderful tool. We can look at our situation, take time to study the Word, take time for thanksgiving and bring our heart into line with what God wants to do. Then we craft a prayer that covers the whole issue. Write your prayers out, over and over, until you feel them seep into your heart. Write them with your friends, helping one another, learning from one another and inspiring one another. Then commit yourself to praying the crafted prayer.[11] Graham Cooke, *Crafted Prayer*

Deeper Still Life Application
How to Write a Crafted Prayer

You want to go deeper in spiritual insight when you pray. We've just read about praying with insight, enthroning God through prayer mapping, and writing crafted prayers. In this exercise you will practice writing your own crafted prayer. Be sure to give yourself plenty of time because you want to be still enough to hear God's voice. Find a quiet place, get a notebook and pen, and do the following:

- Begin with thanksgiving and worship - Read and pray the Psalms and other Scripture, thanking God for what He has done in your life. You may want to pray Psalm 100.

- Become still and prepare your heart to listen to God - I try to take an hour each afternoon to be still before God, listening to what He wants to say to me. It is a highlight of my life. Read Psalm 46.

- Ask the Lord to show you what He wants to accomplish in your situation - Bring your circumstances to God and ask Him questions. Ask Him to work in your life during this time.

- Write down any thoughts and words God gives you - This is where a journal is very valuable. You can look back and see patterns, similar thoughts, ideas, and words.

- Pray for further clarification - Take these words and thoughts back to the Lord in prayer. Write down any further insight you may receive.

- In stillness, craft a prayer - Don't rush writing a crafted prayer because it takes time. Include the key words, thoughts, ideas, and Scriptures that God has given you.

- Take your crafted prayer back to God - Ask for confirmation. You may do this over time until you are confident that you have the mind of God on how to pray. This may take time—moments, hours, days or weeks—because God may continue to add clarification to your crafted prayer.

- Pray a prayer of faith and proclamation over what God will do through your prayers - When you believe you know the will of God over your situation, your confidence and faith will rise to a new level.

How to Help Others Write Crafted Prayers

Get together with an individual or group. Before you meet, inform each person that they will be writing a crafted prayer. This gives them time to think about it. Have them bring their journal or pen and paper when you meet. Study the section in this chapter on crafted prayer before beginning. Answer any questions.

Begin with a time of worship and praise. Then go through the life application points before giving each one 30-60 minutes to begin writing a crafted prayer. Have a time of sharing what God has been showing each one, and end by praying a prayer of faith and proclamation over what God will do. Realize that God will help you develop this prayer and that it may take time, but this was a good initial step.

My Prayer to God

Lord, I enter Your gates with thanksgiving and Your courts with praise. I give thanks to You and praise Your name. For You are good and Your love endures forever, Your faithfulness continues through all generations (Psalm 100:5). I pray that You will teach me how to pray with spiritual insight. I ask for insight that is beyond my understanding. I want my prayers to be initiated by Your Spirit. Help me to be discerning and sharp-sighted as I pray. I ask that you would give me a spirit of wisdom and revelation in the knowledge of You, that the eyes of my understanding would be enlightened, that I might know the hope of my calling and the exceeding greatness of Your power towards me (Ephesians 1:17-19). Enlighten the eyes of my heart.

Help me to write crafted prayers so that I can pray with boldness and assurance over situations in my life. Help me to be purposeful and intentional in my prayers. Teach me to wait and listen to You. Show me how to pray with insight for my family, friends, and workplace. I want to align my requests with Your will. Teach me to pray prayers that are initiated in heaven. I thank You that You will take me deeper in spiritual insight. "The beginning of wisdom is this: Get wisdom. Though it cost all you have, get understanding. Cherish her and she will exalt you; embrace her, and she will honor you" (Proverbs 4:7-8). Lord, I pray for wisdom and understanding. In Jesus' name, amen.

CHAPTER SIX

DEEPER IN DISCIPLINING THE SOUL

Trust in him at all times, you people;
pour out your hearts to him,
for God is our refuge.
Psalm 62:8

I WAS DEEPLY TOUCHED by his testimony as he stood before us blindly at the Franklin Graham Festival in Virginia. There was a beautiful sense of godliness and brokenness in his voice—a peace, strength and confidence in God—that touched the hearts of everyone present.

On April 6, 2005 U.S. Army Captain Scott Smiley found a parked vehicle on a road he used almost every day. It looked suspicious so he parked several yards away and yelled to the driver to get out of his car. The man raised his arms up and started coming forward. What should Captain Scott do? He shot in front of the man to show him that he meant business. The man stopped, raised his hands in the air, and then came forward.

Suddenly there was a loud boom!

Captain Smiley woke up two weeks later at Walter Reed Army Medical Center in Washington D.C. He couldn't move his right side. He was blinded because of a car bomb that exploded while he was serving in Iraq. The doctor told him that he would be blind for the rest of his life.

Army Captain Scott Smiley's faith has been severely tested. He went through a dark night of the soul in every dimension of his life. He will never, ever see again. He probably knows more than any of us what it means to pray with desperation a prayer of lament.

Captain Smiley and his wife were shipped out to Palo Alto, California to a blind rehabilitation center. It was there that he realized that his life belonged to God. It wasn't up to him to decide what to do with his life or where to go. It was up to Jesus Christ. Through the discipline of the soul, he has learned to praise God every day. He had learned how to face the discipline of hiddenness. He has found Jesus as his answer in even the darkest moments of his life.

You may not be blind or encountering anything like Captain Smiley, but you may be going through some difficult personal experience of your own. You may be wondering, "How can I find it through the dark night of the soul just as Army Captain Smiley did? How can I learn to pray honest prayers where I can pour out my heart to God in a meaningful way?" In this chapter learn how to face the dark night of the soul and how to pray an honest prayer of lament. Let's discover how to get the most out of the discipline of hiddenness.

The Dark Night of the Soul

John of the Cross, a 16th century believer, coined this term to describe a unique kind of spiritual suffering. Distinct from the pain God's children feel when their fellowship with Him is broken because of sin, this sense of darkness seems actually to be inflicted by God in order to do a deeper work in those who long for more of Him. By stripping us of things we've come to rely upon—even good things like answers to prayer, or feelings of joy, or experiences of His presence—God brings us to a new place where we know and love Him for who He is alone.[1] Tracey McCary Rhodes, "Clinging to God in the Darkness"

The dark night of the soul is a common occurrence to all who are seeking hard after God.

I wish I had understood it many years ago when Norm and I entered into a season of darkness that lasted several years. We had spent many years on the mission field, traveling to more than 65 countries during that time. But suddenly—and almost without warning—we came home and entered into a long, dark night of the soul. During the few years before leaving our overseas work, I had experienced a severe sleep problem that probably lasted for about ten years. We were getting worn out through our years of intensive ministry overseas, and our personal problems were increasing.

One of our mission's leaders gave us some sound counsel and said that maybe we should go home and take a break from overseas work for a while. And this we did.

But we never anticipated the dark night we would face when we returned to our own country. We had time on our hands—we were confused after so much continuous traveling—and we were like strangers in our own land, feeling lonely and lost. This dark night of the soul lasted for several years. There were many days where I cried out to God for help and understanding. We felt as if our entire life had been dismantled, with the thought that it may never be erected again. There were days when we felt like totally giving up.

But God has his hand in the entire darkness that we faced. It was all in his absolutely perfect design. I didn't understand at the time what was happening to us, but now in looking back, I see it as the most important time in our spiritual journey with God. It not only brought us personally into a depth with God that we had never known before, it has been the key and the stepping stone into the ministries we are now involved in called Elijah Company, Inc. and Intercessors Arise International. The Bible says in John 12:24 (Amplified):

> *I assure you, most solemnly I tell you, unless a grain of wheat falls into the earth and dies, it remain [just one grain; it never becomes more but lives] by itself alone. But if it dies, it produces many others and yields a rich harvest.*

In order to bring us deeper, God needs to strip us of ourselves. He needs to remove all the wisdom and ways of the world, all the sense of human accomplishment we may have felt in our ministry, and all of our nervous energy and soulish activity. He wants to draw us to Himself alone, and He will even take away the good things in order to give us the best.

Although this time may seem bewildering, God has His perfect plan, and He knows in every moment what He is doing. He lets us experience a dry and lonely desert experience where He, alone, sustains our spiritual life. He works deeply within and teaches us the ways of the Spirit.

Moses, Job, Joseph, Paul, and a number of Biblical characters went through a dark night of the soul. This is where they learned valuable spiritual truths. This is where they went deeper in disciplining the soul. This is a special class in the school of God's Spirit from which we gain much spiritual strength for whatever we do for God in the future. It is personalized with our name on it and is designed to change us from the inside out. It is a choice place to be. In her book, *Requirements for Greatness*, Lori Wilke gives us insight about Jewish potters:

> When Jewish potters make new pots, they set aside the very best pots and pottery for special treatment. After they put their name on the underside of these extra good pieces, they put them away in a cold, damp room for storage, away from the public view. It is only when the more selective buyers ask for the "very best" of the potter's products that the craftsman will retrieve the chosen pots from their hidden storage place.[2]

The dark night of the soul is the most difficult experience for each one of us. God doesn't seem to tell us what we are going through. It would be easy if He would just say, "This is only a test." It seems as if our life has reached a place where there is no way out except God. This is where He wants us. It's a place of absolute dependence when we are at the very end of our human ability and resources.

I remember this dark night well. It has become a memorial in my everyday experience for I was marked for life by the lessons I learned during those days and years of loneliness and loss. It is the place where we find our deepest treasure and where we find true hope in God alone. It is the place where we are set free from ourselves in a deeper way.

The dark night of the soul has been the place where our life ministry was truly birthed in all its fullness. I must admit that it was extremely difficult each and every day, and it seemed as if that dark season would never end. But God always knows what He was doing. He is developing a hidden place where true faith and fruitfulness is birthed.

But how do we face it successfully?

How to Face the Dark Night of the Soul

> Proven vessels have been oven-baked and refired again and again in the kiln of commitment until they've proven their ability to withstand the pressures and temperature of the fire. Once you cry out, "God, I want to be like you," then you will probably be broken up, made over into a brand-new vessel, and whisked out of the bright light into a deserted and dark back storage room until the appointed time. Remember, diamonds were just pieces of coal formed in a dark, pressurized environment.[3] Lori Wilke, *Requirements for Greatness*

There are ways to get the greatest benefit when facing the dark night of the soul. When you go through this season when the heavens seem silent and all seems dark, you can access an untapped reservoir of grace. You can hold onto raw faith and trust that God knows what He is doing. He will help you day by day as you apply these principles to your life.

- **Trust God and rely on Him.** You may feel that you made some mistake during this dark time, but God is really maturing you spiritually.

- **Study the Biblical characters.** Realize that they spent time in the desert. Study the lives of Moses, Elijah, David, John the Baptist, and Paul. All of them experienced the dark night of the soul.

- **Obey God and walk in repentance.** Let Him touch every single area of your life with His refining fire. Repent as He lets the weaknesses and sin in your life come to the surface.

- **Cling to God and His Word.** He is the one who will carry you through this season of your life. Don't hurry it along, but learn to cling to God—even when He seems far away. Hold onto Scriptural promises.

- **Thank God for this hidden place.** Recognize that it is a necessary part of your growth. Character is not developed overnight. There will come a time where you are eternally grateful for this season in your life. Thank Him now.

- **Wait on God in persistent prayer.** Keep on pursuing God, and cry out to Him in persistent prayer. Wait on Him for He has an appointed time to release you.

- **Love God for who He is.** Learn to be a lover of God for Himself and not for what He can give you. Worship and praise Him throughout the day.

- **Recommit your soul to God afresh.** Don't give up or complain. It will only lengthen this time. Commit your life afresh to God's purposes and plans. Allow Him to re-fashion your life according to His design.

I thank God for every day I spent in the dark night of the soul. Without it, I could never do what I am doing today. It was the hardest time in my life, but it changed me forever. Now I treasure the seclusion I learned during that season of my life. I can now look forward in a new way to desert moments when God brings me alone in His presence, because I know how He is deepening the quality of my life. I have learned to pray honest prayers of lament during these times. I can embrace my present problems as I wait for God's deliverance because of learning these lessons in the dark.

> *Who among you fears the LORD and obeys the word of his servant? Let the one who walks in the dark, who has no light, trust in the name of the LORD and rely on their God* (Isaiah 50:10).

Through the dark night God brings forth the brightest faith, the greatest freedom, and a diamond that could be formed in no other way. He brings us deeper in a hidden lifestyle. This really is one of the big secrets to a deeper prayer life. And it's not just for us alone, but through it we can bring blessing to others. For those of you who are facing a dark night, I encourage you to embrace this season for you will truly receive memorial stones that will change you forever for God's glory and for your greatest good.

A glorious dawn awaits you.

> I know now that for every dark night, a glorious dawn awaits. Wherever you may be in your spiritual journey, I pray that this truth will encourage you to reach for all God is, regardless of the

cost. He will not hide Himself from you even one minute beyond His sovereign plan. He holds you, even when you feel completely deserted, and He's shedding His love into your heart. Cling to Him through the darkness. The trials that overwhelm right now will one day appear as memorial stones—monuments that testify to His great love and power to redeem. This is the legacy of the soul's dark night.[4] Tracey McCary Rhodes, "Clinging to God in the Darkness"

The Prayer of Lament

It seems to me that we do not need to be taught how to lament since we have so many models in Scripture. What we need is simply the assurance that it's okay to lament. We all carry deep within ourselves a pressurized reservoir of tears. It takes only the right key at the right time to unlock them. In God's perfect time, these tears can be released to form a healing flood. That's the beauty and the mystery of the prayer of lament.[5] Michael Card

Did you know that even in sadness you can worship God in prayer?

You can worship God in the midst of difficulty through a prayer of lament. There are many of these kinds of prayers in Scripture, and all the major Bible characters prayed prayers of lament to God. This is a type of prayer that we rarely hear about, yet at times, it is a necessary part of each one of our prayer lives.

When experiencing the dark night of the soul, prayers of lament are so helpful. We live in a broken world where things do not always go right. There are times when we don't know what God is doing or which way to turn.

Bringing before God a prayer of lament can make all the difference in the world, because God actually changes us during these times when we pour out our hearts to Him in lament. Prayers of lament are a form of worship and faith. We worship God even in the midst of pouring our difficulty out before Him. Instead of backing away from God during a hard time or a dark night, we face the pain and worship Him with it. As an act of love, we offer it all to God. We lay everything before His Throne.

> Lamentation is a powerful, and meaningful, form of worship be-
> cause it places our love for God above even the worst of circum-
> stances in our life… God does not ask us to deny the existence of
> our suffering. He does want us to collect it, stand in those things
> and make Him an offering. The Holy Spirit, our Comforter, helps
> us to do this: He aligns Himself with our will and says, "I will help
> you to will to worship God." The glory of the majesty of God is
> that He helps us will and do.[6] Graham Cooke, *Drawing Close*

Let me give you an example of a song of lament that has touched many of us throughout the years. The Spafford family lost everything they owned in a fire. Making plans to rebuild, they moved from Chicago to France. Horatio Spafford carefully planned the trip from America to France and booked tickets on a huge ship for his wife and four daughters. He was planning to join them a few weeks later. On the voyage, the ship was rammed by another vessel and sank, carrying his wife and four daughters to the bottom of the ocean. All his plans suddenly were crushed.

In grief and lament as his ship passed over the watery grave of his wife and four beloved daughters, he wrote this famous hymn, "It is Well With My Soul".[7] Many of us know that hymn and have been touched deeply through the words expressed in every verse. Horatio Spafford knew the power of the prayer of lament in that instant. His words have helped multitudes face their own sorrows.

He refused to let God go in the midst of difficulty and grief.

Prayers of lament may look like prayers of complaining, but they can still be prayers of faith because this type of prayer refuses to let God go even in the hard times. God may seem absent, but He is not. Prayers of lament are honest before God and bring us face to face with Him as we try to understand what is going on in our heart. Job was one who prayed deep prayers of lament. He had lost everything—his family, friends, home, and health. Yet he wrestled through with God and clung to Him as he sought for meaning to his struggles. He held onto His faith in God and turned to Him with all his heart. He wanted to see God in the midst of his pain. Job did not let God go. He said:

I know that my Redeemer lives, and that in the end he will stand upon the earth. And after my skin has been destroyed, yet in my flesh I will see God; I myself will see him with my own eye—I, and not another. How my heart yearns within me! (Job 19:25-27).

In the end God gave him back so much more. Job was able to see God in a far deeper way than before his trial. Not letting go and bringing our heart to God in the midst of pain is an act of faith. Well-known musician, Michael Card tells us how we can learn faith from Job's prayer of lament:

> Finally, we see in Job one of the most fundamental lessons we can learn from lament: that protesting and even accusing God through the prayers of lament is, nevertheless, an act of faith. The lament of faith does not deny the existence of God. Rather, it appeals to God on the basis of his loving kindness, in spite of current conditions that suggest otherwise. Job simply would not let go of God—in spite of death, disease, isolation, and ultimately, a fear that God has abandoned him.[8]

How to Write a Prayer of Lament

Habakkuk 3:17-18 is a well-known example of a prayer of lament. Habakkuk was living in difficult circumstances but through a prayer of lament, he was brought to a place of peace. In chapter one his prayer was prayed in frustration; he was asking God "how long" and "why" regarding his circumstances. He was not denying the existence of pain. He was bringing it before God. Perhaps the situation sounds similar to our day.

Why do you make me look at injustice? Why do you tolerate wrongdoing? Destruction and violence are before me; there is strife, and conflict abounds. Therefore the law is paralyzed, and justice never prevails. The wicked hem in the righteous, so that justice is perverted" (Habakkuk 1:3-4).

Through Habakkuk's prayer of lament, God changed his heart. He didn't immediately change his situation. God had directed his attention to His long-range plans and not the present circumstances he was facing. He told Habakkuk to wait and to live by faith. By the last chapter he prayed:

LORD, I have heard of your fame; I stand in awe of your deeds, LORD. Repeat them in our day, in our time make them known; in wrath remember mercy (Habakkuk 3:2).

Though his circumstances were difficult, God met with Habakkuk in his prayer and changed his heart. He began to see from a new perspective. He began to put his faith in God's eternal hope, and his prayer of lament was a form of worship to God. In lamenting, you actually worship God with your sorrow. We read in Habakkuk 3:17-18:

<u>Though</u> the fig tree does not bud and there are no grapes on the vines, though the olive crop fails and the fields produce no food, though there are no sheep in the pen and no cattle in the stalls, <u>yet</u> I will rejoice in the LORD, I will be joyful in God my Savior.

You may want to write down your own prayer of lament using the words "though" and "yet" to begin to phrase your lament. Do this when you are facing difficulty. Save this exercise in prayer for the hard moments in your life.

- **Find a quiet place with God.** Being alone with Him is a necessity for this kind of prayer.

- **Ask the Holy Spirit to guide you.** He will lead you in a prayer of lament. He will open up your heart to God.

- **Be in God's presence.** We are often so much in a hurry but a prayer of lament takes time spent in God's presence. Give yourself wholly to God.

- **Write down the "though" circumstances in your life.** What difficulties and challenges are you right now facing? What pain or grief do you feel? These are the "though" circumstances.

- **Offer these things to God.** Offer God the hard things as a sacrifice. Don't ask for anything.

- **Worship God by completing the phrase.** "Though these things have happened, yet _____." Worship God in a series of yet statements. Bless and praise Him even in spite of the difficult things.

I guarantee that this will have a great effect on your life. You go deeper in the discipline of the soul.

I had some very difficult moments in my life in 2005 and 2006. I was facing cancer, several surgeries, and a lengthy recovery. I learned that through pouring out my heart to God in prayers of lament, my heart was changed. I began to look at things in a much more positive light.

Praising God in the midst of difficulty is so powerful because, as the following quote says, God stands in the moment with us. The thing that I can testify during those moments of difficulty—when I brought my pain directly to God and walked with Him through it—was the reality that God was really there.

God stands in the moment with you. God gives you a deeper revelation of Himself.

> If you are in mourning, you have the opportunity to worship in the most powerful way possible: lamentation. This worship isn't done in order to have God remove the pain. It simply recognizes that God stands in the moment with us. Lamentation elevates God in the presence of our enemies. It brings out a side of God that other forms of worship simply cannot touch.[9] Graham Cooke, *Drawing Close*

The Discipline of Hiddenness

> We need to learn to stay in the place of hiddenness, in God's presence, until we receive everything that God has for us during that time. It is easy to break off from hiddenness too soon. In our hearts we may secretly feel that manifestation is the ultimate thing and that hiddenness is the second best. In reality, there is no difference between the two—they are both brilliant! You just have to learn to live in them both... There is a discipline attached to being hidden with God, and you have to learn the joy of the discipline, staying there until God moves you on.[10] Graham Cooke, *When the lights Go Out*

There is an abundant life that comes from the hidden place. Most of us find this hard to believe because we associate it with pain and loss. We do go through these things, but if we see hiddenness from God's perspective, it can totally change how we walk through it. I've already written about the dark night of the soul, a time where we face the discipline of hiddenness. But let's look at this discipline more closely and why it is so important in going deeper in prayer and in our relationship with God.

In going through these times as I began to understand them more fully, I have learned to thank God, knowing that He was changing me on the inside. I learned not to look at what everyone else was doing who were in a period of God's manifest blessing, but I concentrated on what God was doing in me. Learning the discipline of hiddenness can become the place of greatest breakthrough in your life.

> Developing an ongoing walk with God by the power of the Holy Spirit is a discipline. Practicing faith is a discipline. Hiddenness is God's way of establishing these disciplines in your life. Once established, they prevent the enemy from invading your life and touching you, because regardless of your emotions, you know how to find the presence of God; you have a constant assurance of His presence and His commitment to you.[11] Graham Cooke, *When the lights Go Out*

There is an advantage to going deeper in a hidden lifestyle. Disciplining ourselves and learning how to get the utmost out of this season in our life is a key to our success. It is here that we can tap into the Christ-like life of real abundance. The word "abundance" in Webster's Dictionary means: "great plenty, an overflowing quality, ample sufficiency, fullness, abundant supply, plentiful"[12]

Hiddenness leads us into the overflowing, abundant life that we have in Christ. God's people are meant to walk in abundance. They are ones who go deep with God and must learn how to stand in His presence where the enemy cannot defeat or destroy. It is in this hidden place where we find the all-sufficiency of God even when He may seem hidden.

He is there as we look with the eyes of faith and expectation.

While living on the ship called *Doulos*, I remember a time when someone gave Norman and I an unusual gift of a caterpillar. That caterpillar quickly spun a cocoon. We put it by our tiny porthole of light in our dark cabin home. It sat there lifeless for days and weeks. We almost threw it away, thinking that it certainly must be dead. But one day when we entered our cabin and turned on the light, there to our surprise was a beautiful butterfly. That caterpillar had no resemblance to the butterfly. In that hidden place God had transformed it into a totally new creature. A metamorphose had taken place.

This so reminds me of how God transforms us in the time of hiddenness. When we go through those seasons something supernatural takes place. We become new. We read in 2 Corinthians 5:17: *Therefore, if anyone is in Christ, the new creation has come: The old has gone, the new is here!* In times of hiddenness God does a transforming work within us. Nobody knows about it because we are hidden. But one day we become like that beautiful, colorful butterfly.

Through hiddenness we move into a place of abundance.

How can we get the most out of these times when we are learning to walk in a greater dimension of faith? How can we learn the abundant life from seasons of hiddenness? Like the example of Army Captain Scott Smiley, there are ways that we can get the most out of times where we are going deeper in the discipline of the soul. Finding God's rest and peace in the midst of difficult experiences becomes a weapon against the enemy. Yielding inwardly moment by moment to God and finding His presence is a much greater alternative than dwelling on the difficulties in our lives.

During seasons of hiddenness we need to praise God, and focus on His majesty and sovereignty. Remember that Captain Smiley learned to worship God even though he was blind. What an amazing testimony. He actually learned to see God in a greater dimension than those of us who actually have our eyes. He learned the discipline of living in God's presence every day.

As followers of Jesus, let's go *deeper still* in the discipline of knowing God than we ever have before. God wants to take each one of us deeper into a hidden lifestyle. He wants to bring us into the place of abundance.

I believe that hiddenness is one of the most exciting disciplines that we can learn in the realm of the Spirit. When you learn how to access it and live it, suddenly everything makes sense. Everything falls to you. All the things that come against you only enable you to go deeper into God, because you have learned the discipline of living in His presence. A man involved in hidden-ness, looking for meaning, is a delight to the Lord.[13] Graham Cooke, *When the lights Go Out*

Deeper Still Life Application
How to Benefit from a Season of Hiddenness

How can we access the wisdom of God in the hidden place? The following are a few key things to keep in mind on this journey. Take time to sit silently in God's presence. Meditate on seasons in your life when God has kept you in the hidden place or you have faced the dark night of the soul. You may be in this season presently, or you may evaluate a previous season of hiddenness. These points are in the present tense and will help to guide you in this season. If you are evaluating a previous time, think about how you applied this to your life then, and write down your successes and failures.

- Stay hidden until God moves you out - If you move too fast, you will miss something of what God wants to do in your life. There will be a tendency to want to move too soon. Receive everything you can from the Lord during this time.

- Focus on worshipping God - Set your personal problems and circumstances aside. The place of worship brings forth trust and faith.

- Don't look to your feelings but live in your faith - You may feel perplexed because you are learning to perceive things differently and from a new level. Don't let that perplexity move you. God will bring you into the light in His time. Cast out all doubt in Jesus' name.

- Expect to receive a deeper revelation of God - Live with expectation. God is teaching you spiritual wisdom that is so different than the world system. He is teaching you about Himself.

- Expect God to change you - What He gives you during a time of hiddenness will change you forever. He is teaching you to analyze things in the spirit and not in the soul. This is a time of personal enlargement in God.

- Expect God to reveal to you strategies to overcome obstacles in your life - It is in the place of rest that He can reveal to you strategies that will overcome any situation. Ask God your questions. Expect Him to show you new truth to overcome difficulties in your life.

- Thank God for this time of hiddenness - Become preoccupied with God. Offer Him worship, praise, and thanksgiving on a daily basis. This will overcomes the power of the enemy in your life.

If you are facing a difficulty or going through the dark night of the soul, you may want to write a prayer of lament. Prayerfully do the exercise in this chapter called "How to Write a Prayer of Lament."

How to Help Others
Benefit from a Season of Hiddenness

Get together with an individual or group and go through this exercise on hiddenness. Have a discussion on hiddenness with each one sharing how they reacted during a season of hiddenness. You may want to point out some of the key points in this teaching by briefly go through the three parts of this chapter. Listen carefully to any who are presently going through hiddenness or the dark night of the soul, and pray specifically for those individuals. This discussion can lead to a greater openness and personal honesty in sharing. Encourage any going through difficult life circumstances to write a prayer of lament as outlined in this chapter. End with praying the following prayer.

My Prayer to God

Lord, I thank you that you want to teach me about hiddenness. I pray that you will give me wisdom in the secret place and faith to behold you at all times. Hide me in the secret place of Your presence. Your hand is on my life when I am facing a time of hiddenness. You are always with me, and Your Holy Spirit helps me. I ask for peace in Your presence. Change me internally to become more like You. Help me to respond in the right way during times of hiddenness. Give me a deeper revelation of You, and show me new strategies for my life. I thank you for the dark night of the soul. I thank you for these seasons in my life where you strip me of myself and teach me dependence on You. Help me to trust and rely on You. Teach me to cling to You and Your Word as I learn to wait on You. Help me not to complain but worship You when I go through difficulty. I want to understand what is going on in my heart during the hard times in my life. Teach me to offer You the hard things as a sacrifice.

My soul will find rest because You are my rock and my salvation. Because You are my fortress, I will not be shaken. You are my mighty rock, my refuge (Psalm 62:5-7). "Though the fig tree does not bud and there are no grapes on the vines, though the olive crop fails and the fields produce no food, though there are no sheep in the pen and no cattle in the stalls, yet I will rejoice in the LORD, I will be joyful in God my Savior" (Habakkuk 3:17-18). In Jesus' name, amen.

CHAPTER SEVEN

DEEPER IN EFFECTIVE PRAYER

*The prayer of a righteous person
is powerful and effective.*
James 5:16b

WE MET TOGETHER EVERY MORNING at 9:00 A.M. It was a small group of wives who had a special burden to pray for the people on board the *Doulos*.

Most of the ship's personnel were young people from countries all over the world, giving their lives for two years on board a ship that sailed from nation to nation spreading the good news of Jesus. They came with their joys and sorrows, some carrying a heavy load of emotional baggage from the past. Others came to change the world but discovered that it wasn't as easy as they expected. *Doulos* life required a high degree of commitment and a level of ruggedness that many had not bargained for. But they came, and through the ups and downs of ship life and spiritual warfare on the high seas, they changed and developed spiritually.

It was this group of wives who prayed faithfully for these individuals to grow and become more Christ-like through the everyday challenges of life on board God's ship. They were like the ship's engine—keeping things going effectively through their daily prayers—being on watch daily for enemy attack and rejoicing when the battles were won.

Once a year there is a Sabbath week on board the ship when all work is shut down except for the bare minimum to keep the ship running. All programs are stopped and everyone seeks God on a deeper level. A guest speaker is invited to the ship to speak for a week on a designated theme.

During the Sabbath week there is more time for prayer and waiting on God, and there is an open time of sharing testimonies and what God has been doing in one's life on the inside. This is a special time of re-commitments—a time of strengthening unity among one another and with God. It is an unforgettable week for everyone on board.

On this Sabbath week as the testimonies were shared, the wives secretly rejoiced as they saw one by one share how God had been working in their life.

A breakthrough in prayer, a breakthrough in relationships or in family relationships at home, a development in faith and trusting God, forgiving one another—so many wonderful testimonies were shared. It was not a coincidence, as the wives realized that most of them were accomplished through effective prayer for each one. The on-target prayers accomplished great things through persevering prayer. Some problems had seemed insurmountable, but God had answered in the impossible place. God answered fervent prayer.

You may ask, "How can I be effective in prayer just like this group of praying wives on the *Doulos*? How can I see power in my prayer life in an impossible situations?" In this chapter discover the power of possibility in the impossible place. Find out how to persevere in prayer and break through any hindrances you may have in your prayer life.

The Power of Possibility
in an impossible Place

All thoughts of holiness are God's; all manner of loving-kindness and tender mercies are His. All weaknesses are made for us so that we might be in a place of absolute helplessness, for when we are weak, than we are strong (2 Corinthians 12:10). All divine acquaintances with Him today will put us in the place where we may be the broken, empty vessel ready for Christ's use.[1] Smith Wigglesworth

Have you ever felt like you were in an impossible place? Have you ever felt like you were praying for the impossible? There is a power of God that is released in the impossible place. God is looking for faith, and real faith has to do with the impossible.

Learn to pray impossible prayers. Learn to launch out into the deep and pray God-sized prayers. This is one of the secrets to a deeper prayer life. God loves it when we pray for the impossible, when we believe Him for things that are beyond our abilities. He is looking for those with faith who will still press through in prayer when the going seems absolutely impossible. Sometimes it may seem difficult to see how you can make it to the very end, but He is the God of the impossible.

A little girl was taking a long journey on a train. Her train had to cross many rivers. Every time she saw the water in advance, she was fearful. She could not see how the train would cross the water and make it to the other side. But as they approached the river, suddenly a bridge would appear and the train would safely go over the river. This happened over and over during her trip. The little girl finally leaned back and sighed a long breath of relief. She finally could trust her situation. She excitedly said to the person next to her:

Somebody has put bridges for us all the way!

Isn't this a good reminder for us? We are not alone in life. God has built bridges for us all the way. The way may look impossible at the moment, but God has a way through the difficulty where we can cross over to a new place and get to our destination through faith-filled prayer.

We are involved in training cross-cultural workers to go to the nations. One thing that I always stress with individuals in regard to their personal destiny is this: Believe God for something that is bigger than what you can personally accomplish. We each must learn to pray for the impossible on a regular basis. We must learn to believe God for something that is greater than anything we can achieve. We must let our faith be tested to the very core. We must each pray for something that is bigger than ourselves.

We are earthen vessels but God is mighty and great. We need to raise our view of Him and realize that He is able to do the impossible. It is right in the midst of the impossibility that God will be highly exalted.

But we have this treasure in jars of clay to show that this all-surpassing power is from God and not from us (2 Corinthians 4:7).

He loves the impossible place in our lives, because it is here that He will show His supreme greatness. E. M. Bounds writes about the possibilities of prayer:

The possibilities of prayer are the possibilities of faith. Prayer and faith are Siamese twins. One heart animates them both. Faith is always praying. Prayer is always believing. Faith must have a tongue by which it can speak. Prayer is the tongue of faith. Faith must receive. Faith is the hand of faith stretched out to receive. Prayer must rise and soar. Faith must give prayer the wings to fly and ascend. Prayer must have an audience with God. Faith opens the door, and access and audience are given. Prayer asks. Faith lays its hand on the thing asked for.[2]

Several things happen in our lives when we face the impossible place. We often do not like to be challenged in this way, but God does a deep work within us when we face the impossible with persevering faith. The Apostle Paul learned to delight in the impossible place, because he realized that it was there that he experienced the true power of God. This is what happens:

- **We lose control.** We are divinely sustained by a power greater than ourselves. When we lose our own control, then we experience the power of Christ's control.

  Therefore I will boast all the more gladly about my weaknesses, so that Christ's power may rest on me (2 Corinthians 12:9).

- **We become absolutely dependent.** We are weak, and He is strong. We become broken vessels, empty and ready for Christ to use.

  That is why for Christ's sake, I delight in weaknesses, in insults, in hardships, in persecutions, in difficulties. For when I am weak, then I am strong (2 Corinthians 12:10).

- **We are changed.** We move into the place where God is on the throne of our lives, and it changes us. When we are changed, we can change other things. We lose our identity in Christ, and it is He that is living through us.

I have been crucified with Christ and I no longer live, but Christ lives in me. The life I now live in the body, I live by faith in the Son of God, who loved me and gave himself for me (Galatians 2:20).

- **We cease from our own works.** We give place to God's ways and His work. We become an instrument of noble purposes.

In a large house there are articles not only of gold and silver, but also of wood and clay; some are for special purposes and some for common use. Those who cleanse themselves from the latter will be instruments for special purposes, made holy, useful to the Master and prepared to do any good work (2 Timothy 2:20-21).

- **We rest in faith.** God teaches us to rest in faith, and we learn to enter His rest. This means that we cease from our own fleshly works.

There remains, then, a Sabbath-rest for the people of God; for anyone who enters God's rest also rests from their own work, just as God did from His (Hebrews 4:10).

Do you think it was easy for the Apostle Paul to live in the impossible place? Was it easy for Paul to become weak and lose control? Was it easy for a high achiever to cease from his works and rest in faith?

No! He had to learn to live in this way. In the natural, he was strong and had great ability in so many areas. He was a high achiever, a very gifted and capable man. He was intelligent and able to do great things. But God touched him deeply, and he learned to live a crucified life. He learned to count everything as rubbish that He might gain Christ and be found in Him (Philippians 3:8). He learned to lose control and become absolutely dependent so that God could be in control and do the impossible through him.

Perhaps you are like most of us. There are situations in your life that call for the power of God. You are in an impossible place. You may have an impossible, God-sized dream, and you can't do it or see it happen in your own strength. There is the need to pray for something that is absolutely impossible in the natural realm.

Don't give up. God loves the impossible place. He is taking you deeper in effective prayer because this kind of prayer always involves faith. Keep on praying for in due season He will show Himself strong on your behalf. He loves to answer impossible prayers of faith. Fervently pray for your dreams and for God to break through the impossible place, because He can move any mountain.

With God all things are possible.

> And Jesus, replying, said to them, "Have faith in God [constantly]. Truly I tell you, whoever says to this mountain, Be lifted up and thrown into the sea! and does not doubt at all in his heart but believes that what he says will take place, it will be done for him" (Mark 11:22-23, Amplified).

Perseverance in Prayer

Prayer must be clothed with fervency, strength, and power. It is the force that, centered on God, determines the amount of Himself given out for earthly good. Men who are fervent in spirit are bent on attaining righteousness, truth, grace, and all other sublime, powerful graces that adorn the character of the authentic, unquestioned child of God.[3] E. M. Bounds, *E. M. Bounds on Prayer*

Are you persistently seeking God in prayer? Are you like Jacob who said, "I will not let you go unless you bless me?" God likes it when we wrestle with Him in prayer because it is a passionate activity. It takes perseverance in order to be effective in prayer. It is amazing how perseverance and endurance in prayer brings everything else in line in our lives. Chaos turns into peace, confusion turns into rest, and despair turns into joy.

I have had people ask me, "Does God really answer prayer?"

While on the mission field years ago, one missionary told me he really did not want to pray because he didn't believe that God answers prayer. This individual didn't see the answers to prayer that he was seeking because he was stopping too soon.

I want to assure you that God does answer prayer if we do not give up in fervently pursuing Him in intercession. God waits to see how determined we are in faith. He waits to see if we will not let go until He blesses us. He is looking for fervency and steadfastness, a determination that continues in faith against all odds. He is looking for those who learn to trust regardless of how things may look in the natural.

Victory in any area of life takes perseverance. The McDonalds hamburger chain did not make its first billion dollars for 22 years. IBM took 46 years and Xerox took 63 years to make a billion dollars. We are laying up riches in heaven that are far greater than anything money can buy. Just as these successful companies needed to be persistent, we must be persevering in our prayer lives.

What does it mean to be fervent in prayer?

We read in Webster's Dictionary that fervent means: "to be hot, to boil, to glow, excited, earnest, animated". The word, "fervently" means: "eagerly, with earnest zeal."[4] God is looking for a fervent determination in our prayers. God wants us to be on fire and hot with prayer that perseveres. Fervent prayer may not always be emotional. There are times of quiet intensity and earnest passion inwardly. There are times where we pray in quietness but with steadfast faith. But whether prayer is with or without outward emotion, it expects answers from God. We read in Psalm 119:145:

> *I call with all my heart; answer me, O LORD.*

Like many of you, I am also looking for mighty answers to some big requests regarding a worldwide prayer movement. I know in my heart that God does answer prayer when we do not give up. Even when battling cancer in 2005, I knew in my heart that God was going to break through.

So I continue to persevere daily in my requests. I have determined in my heart that I will not let go until God blesses me. He is looking for character. He is also looking for those who will ask big requests for His glory because He is a big God. So make sure you ask God-sized requests of Him.

The Apostle Paul was not afraid to ask God for big things because he knew that God was able to answer in His own time. His prayers were all consuming. There are many reasons why we should be persevering in prayer like the Apostle Paul. Here are key reasons not to give up:

- **God answers persevering prayer.** Fervent prayer does not give up and is specific with a clear target. God loves to answer these kinds of prayers.

  The effective, fervent prayer of a righteous man avails much (James 5:16, NKJV).

- **God is increasing our faith and will bring reward.** It takes faith to pray sometimes for years for answers to our prayers. We must believe that He will answer and that He is a rewarder of those who diligently seek Him.

  And without faith it is impossible to please God, because anyone who comes to him must believe that he exists and that he rewards those who earnestly seek him (Hebrews 11:6).

- **God is preparing us for the answer.** Most of us are not really ready for the answers to some of our prayers, especially regarding our destiny. We couldn't handle the blessing if it came prematurely. God wants us to be holy. Character is so important to Him.

  But just as he who called you is holy, so be holy in all you do; for it is written: "Be holy, because I am holy" (1 Peter 1:15-16).

- **God cares.** My missionary friend who didn't believe that God answers his prayers was missing out on a big truth about Him, and that is the fact that God cares. He wants to answer our prayers. His love is deep and unfailing.

  But I trust in your unfailing love; my heart rejoices in your salvation. I will sing the LORD's praise, for he has been good to me (Psalm 13:5-6).

There are many ways to help you increase your perseverance in prayer. Praise and worship provide the atmosphere for fervent prayer. Asking others to pray specifically regarding your perseverance, and praying together with others can activate your faith and perseverance. Sensitivity to the Holy Spirit as he leads you in prayer will help you to pray focused, on-target prayers. My faith in prayer increases when I reach out to the lost or go on ministry trips. I see the needs face-to-face. Living a balanced life and getting enough sleep can also help.

As I said earlier, persevering prayer is not always loud or emotional. J. Hudson Taylor, the famous missionary to China, is a great example for us. He established over two hundred mission stations, trained seven hundred Chinese workers, developed a Chinese church of about 125 thousand, baptized nearly fifty thousand Chinese, and helped to bring hundreds of missionaries to the field.

He was a missionary who confessed that his heart many times felt like wood when he prayed. His fervency in prayer was not outward but steadfast. As a result, his inward passion and perseverance in prayer brought great results.

Many of us watch the Olympics in the winter. Why not be in the Olympics with God in your prayer life? Those athletes who make it to the Olympics have practiced over and over again for years. They have learned to persevere when nobody was watching. Most of them have had a passion for one sport, and they have focused on that sport without wavering—whether it is skating, skiing, or swimming.

Can we not do the same in prayer? Can we not make it to the end and get a gold metal at the judgment seat of Christ because of our fervent perseverance in prayer?

I want to affirm your calling in prayer and encourage you to go for the gold. You have a cloud of witnesses in heaven who are right now cheering you on. Go for it! God will answer your prayers here on earth, but the real blessing will be when you reach the finish line and later learn in heaven how God used all your prayers for His eternal purposes.

Like Paul, let us run to win. Perseverance is one of the keys to a deeper prayer life. Can we say like Jacob, "I will not let you go unless you bless me"? Our perseverance in prayer will win the prize.

> Do you not know that in a race all the runners run, but only one gets the prize? Run in such a way as to get the prize. Everyone who competes in the game goes into strict training. They do it to get the crown that will not last; but we do it to get a crown that will last forever. Therefore, I do not fight like a man beating the

air. No, I beat my body and make it my slave so that after I have preached to others, I myself will not be disqualified for the prize (1 Corinthians 9:24-27).

Hindrances to Effective Prayer

This effort to discover the reasons for our leanness in prayer is intended not to discourage praying, but to find the causes underlying our ineffectual prayers and remove them. There is no virtue in continuing grimly to pray on when there are factors present that make our prayers of no effect. We should pray on, but we must pray aright, or our prayers will continue to be fruitless.[5] A. W. Tozer, *The Christian's Handbook*

Have you ever felt a hindrance in your prayer life? Have you ever felt like your prayers were merely hitting the ceiling and not getting through to God?

Because prayer and intercession is so important, each of us must be alert to possible hindrances in our personal prayer lives. We need to be aware of the numerous ways our prayers can be diminished because of personal sin in our lives. We must war for our prayer lives, as a mighty warrior going to battle. You and I are in the greatest of wars against the powers of evil. We must lay aside the sin that so easily entangles us so that we might be the glorious warriors who conquer in the mighty strength of the Lord—with great spiritual power released for His glory.

What are some of the things that can block our prayer lives?

What are the possible hindrances and roadblocks that can get in the way? We need to ask God to search our hearts and show us personally anything that can hinder our intercession. We read in Psalm 139:23-24:

Search me O God, and know my heart; test me and know my anxious thoughts. See if there is any offensive way in me, and lead me in the everlasting way.

In Janet Leighton's article on prayer, she stresses our need to let God search our hearts. She says:

When we pray for God to cleanse our hearts and our motives, it is important to yield the search-and-destroy mission to Him. He is perfectly able to bring wrong motives or any other sinful pattern to our attention and to lead us into repentance.[7]

It is wise for us to carefully consider the following hindrances and meditate on the corresponding Scriptures. Evaluate your own personal life carefully, thoughtfully answer these questions, and ask God to make you a cleansed vessel so that His life can flow through you unhindered.

- **An unforgiving spirit.** Is there anyone I haven't forgiven?

    And when you stand praying, if you hold anything against anyone, forgive them, so that your Father in heaven may forgive you your sins (Mark 11:25).

- **Mistreatment of family members.** Have I mistreated my wife, children, brothers, or sisters? Have I been unloving?

    Husbands, in the same way be considerate as you live with your wives, and treat them with respect as the weaker partner and as heirs with you of the gracious gift of life, so that nothing will hinder your prayers (1 Peter 3:7).

- **Neglecting the poor.** Am I neglecting the poor in any way?

    Whoever shuts their ears to the cry of the poor will also cry out and not be answered (Proverbs 21:13).

- **Idols in the heart.** Is there anything in my life that is taking the place of God?

    Son of man, these men have set up idols in their hearts and put wicked stumbling blocks before their faces. Should I let them inquire of me at all? (Ezekiel 14:3).

- **A wrong motive and selfishness.** Are there any wrong motives in my prayers?

    When you ask, you do not receive, because you ask with wrong motives, that you may spend what you get on your pleasures (James 4:3).

- **Disobedience.** Have I disobeyed God in any way?

  If anyone turns a deaf ear to my instruction, even their prayers are detestable (Proverbs 28:9).

- **Sin in the heart.** Is there sin in any area of my life that is hindering my prayers?

  If I had cherished sin in my heart, the Lord would not have listened; but God has surely listened and has heard my prayer (Psalm 66:18-19).

- **Unbelief.** Do I believe God will answer my prayers?

  But when you ask, he must believe and not doubt, because the one who doubts is like the wave of the sea, blown and tossed by the wind. That person should not expect to receive anything from the Lord. Such a person is double-minded and unstable in all they do (James 1:6-8).

Evelyn Christenson, the founder of United Prayer Ministries and author of numerous books on prayer, tells the story of how she and two other intercessors began to pray together for their church on a weekly basis. They discovered that their own spiritual condition would determine whether God would answer their prayers. They based their prayer meeting on Psalm 66:18 that says: *If I regard iniquity in my heart, the Lord will not hear me.* God began to do a deep work in their personal lives first. Here is what Evelyn said:

> In prayer, we asked God to search our lives for everything that was sin in His sight. For six miserable weeks—to our continuing astonishment—He dug deeper and deeper while we confessed and repented. Finally, at the end of that time, He released us to pray for our church.[8]

The results were astounding. They had thrown off the sin that so easily entangles. For the next six months they had revival in their church because they had been praying for God to cleanse their own lives first, and then they had prayed for their church. We read in Hebrews 12:1:

> *Therefore, since we are surrounded by such a great cloud of witnesses, let us throw off everything that hinders and the sin that*

so easily entangles. And let us run with perseverance the race marked out for us.

I don't think we can fully grasp how powerful and effective prayer is when we remove the hindrances in our own lives. There is potency in prayer that is available to each one of us. God is able to answer prayer most powerfully when there is an open channel of His blessings. He wants to take us deeper in effective prayer. He wants us to be those who are His unhindered channels of blessing everywhere we go. This is powerful.

The Scriptures are clear about the potency of prayer. "The effectual fervent prayer of a righteous man," wrote the inspired James, "availeth much" (James 5:16). With this the whole Bible and Christian experience agree: prayer is effective. When it is not answered, something is wrong. The same apostle who affirmed the effective power of prayer admitted also that prayer is sometimes ineffective: "Ye ask, and receive not, because ye ask amiss, that ye may consume it upon your lusts" (James 4:3). In spite of the difficulties surrounding prayer, it is still the highest activity in which a human being can engage.[9] A. W. Tozer

Deeper Still Life Application
How to Grow in Effective Prayer

We've just looked at the power of possibility in the impossible place, perseverance in prayer, and hindrances to effective prayer. Now look at all three of these areas as you evaluate your effectiveness in prayer. Take time to be quiet before God before starting. With pen and journal in hand, carefully answer these questions and meditate on these Scriptures. Write down any insight the Lord gives you.

- Write a paragraph about any impossible places you are facing presently or have faced recently in your life - In what way is God teaching you dependence in that place? In what way is He changing you? How are you learning to rest in Him? How do you think this impossible place will teach you to be more effective in your prayers? Meditate on 2 Corinthians 12:10; Galatians 2:20; 2 Timothy 2:20-21; and Hebrews 4:10.

- Write a paragraph about how God is teaching you to persevere in your prayers - In what way is He teaching you fervent perseverance in prayer? How is He stretching your faith in prayer? How is He making you holy through this process? How is this making you more effective in your prayers? Meditate on Psalm 62:8; 1 Corinthians 9:24-27; Hebrews 11:6; James 5:16; and 1 Peter 1:15-16.

- Write a paragraph about any possible hindrances in your prayer life - Go through the list of hindrances to prayer in this chapter. Is there anything that is blocking your prayer life and keeping you from effective prayer? Meditate on Psalm 66:18; Ezekiel 14:3; Proverbs 21:13; 28:9; Mark 11:25; Hebrews 12:10; James 1:6-8; 4:3; and 1 Peter 3:7. Confess and repent of any hindrances to effective prayer you see in your life. Receive God's forgiveness. Pray "My Prayer to God."

How to Help Others
Grow in Effective Prayer

Get together with another individual or group, spend a few minutes in worship, and then pray that God guides you in answering these life application questions. Give each person a pen and paper and have them go through the above exercise. Give about 30-60 minutes so that each individual can thoroughly answer these questions.

Come together and have a time of open sharing. Then pray as a group. Bring these things before the Lord and repent whenever necessary. Ask God to help you to grow in your effectiveness in prayer. End with praying the following prayer and thanking God for what He will do.

My Prayer to God

Lord, I want to be powerful and effective in my personal prayer life (James 5:16). I pray that You would search my heart and see if there is any offensive way in me. Show me any possible hindrances in my life to effective prayer. I want to be Your channel of blessing. Reveal to me any sin in my heart, and show me any area of disobedience or unbelief. I choose to believe in the mighty power of prayer every day. You reward those who earnestly seek You (Hebrews 11:6).

I choose to forgive every person that has hurt me. Show me any way that I may have hurt any family members, friends, or co-workers, and give me the grace to ask for forgiveness. Reveal to me any idol in my heart and anything that I may be putting ahead of my relationship with You. Help me to throw off everything that hinders and the sin that so easily entangles, and run with perseverance the race marked out for me. I fix my eyes on You (Hebrews 12:10).

I choose not to neglect prayer. Make my prayers fervent and effective. I want to pray with great faith even in the difficult areas of my lives. Help me to believe You in the impossible place. I pray that you would teach me perseverance in my prayers. I chose to depend and trust in You. "But I trust in your unfailing love; my heart rejoices in your salvation. I will sing the LORD's praise, for he has been good to me" (Psalm 13:5-6). I thank You that "the prayer of a righteous person is powerful and effective" (James 5:16). In Jesus' name, amen.

⚜

CHAPTER EIGHT

DEEPER IN A
FASTING LIFESTYLE

But when you fast, put oil on your head and wash your face,
so that it will not be obvious to men that you are fasting,
but only to your Father, who is unseen;
and your Father, who sees what is done in secret,
will reward you.
Matthew 6:17-18

⚜

HIS FATHER WOULD take bottles of water, go out on the beach, and seek the face of God in extended prayer and fasting for several days. His mother never spent a complete night in sleep because she was up at 3:00 A.M. praying.

Kingsley Fletcher grew up in Africa with parents who strongly believed in the discipline of prayer and fasting. At age six when suffering from a serious eye injury and lying unconscious for three months, the doctors told Kingley's mother, "There is no hope for your son." But she went into serious prayer and fasting, and he miraculously recovered. At ten, Kingsley determined to follow God and at fifteen, he and six other teenagers formed The Power House Evangelistic Ministries.

With a sense of urgency at an early age, he saw the power of prayer and fasting; Kingsley determined to follow his parent's example.

As he watched their lives, he saw how the enemy had to submit to the authority of God. When Christianity first came to their part of Africa, there were no fancy buildings or meeting places. They simply met in the bush, singing praises to God. At times they would pray all night.

When their outdoor crusades were threatened by rain, in faith they commanded the rain to wait until the meetings were over, and they did. At the crusades cripples got up and walked. Blind people were able to see. Miracles were performed in the name of Jesus.

God was doing the miraculous in Africa in answer to simple faith.

> Without great textbooks, much education, or a well-developed theology, God did miracles as a result of a life of seeking the face of God with prayer and fasting. As a result of his parent's example, Kingsley Fletcher is now an internationally known minister, author, businessman, and conference speaker. He is founder and senior pastor of Life Community Church and Kingsley Fletcher Ministries. And this is because he is a man who has dedicated himself to prayer and fasting. He has a fasting lifestyle, and God has rewarded him because of it.[1] Kingsley Fletcher, *Prayer and Fasting*

You may wonder, "How can I grow in my spiritual life in prayer and fasting? How can I see the miraculous power of God in my life just as Kingsley did?" In this chapter discover the purifying power of prayer and fasting. Explore the various fasts in Scripture, and learn to fast the right way with the right heart.

The Purifying Power of Fasting and Prayer

If My people, who are called by My name, will humble themselves and pray and seek My face and turn from their wicked ways, then I will hear from heaven, and I will forgive their sin and will heal their land (2 Chronicles 7:14).

We all need encouragement to practice prayer and fasting. God wants us to go deeper in a fasting lifestyle. It is one of the key ways we will bring in the spiritual harvest wherever we live. I experienced the same example in India as Kingsley did in Africa. After returning from India and being strongly challenged by the pure, humble and simple lives of the Christians I met there, I am convinced that God wants to bring His people into a deep and holy lifestyle. The harvest is ripe in India, and the Christians are positioned in a dedicated lifestyle that is necessary for gathering the lost. They are seeing signs, wonders, and miracles just as they are in Africa.

Realize that fasting and prayer purifies us and makes us ready for harvest.

We may think of fasting as only going without food, but we can fast from anything. You may want to fast sweets, sports, or TV. It is helpful to think of it in terms of a human relationship. When you want to be with your friend, you will cancel all other activities in order to spend time together. It's similar in our relationship with God. It's a way to tell Him that your priority is to be alone with Him and you have decided to cancel your meals, activities, and other important things in order to spend quality time with Him.

Fasting is a wonderful way to seek God wholeheartedly. Bill Bright, founder of Campus Crusade for Christ, made this statement in his book *The Transforming Power of Fasting and Prayer:*

> After 45 years of emphasizing evangelism, discipleship and fulfillment of the Great Commission, some may think I have gone off on a tangent with my strong emphasis on fasting and prayer. The fact is that the best way to help individuals become evangelists for Christ is to bring them into a relationship with God in which the Holy Spirit renews them. Only fasting meets the criteria of each aspect of 2 Chronicles 7:14. When you humble yourself and pray and seek God's face and turn from your wicked ways, something happens to you and you get excited about the Lord in a way that you do not through any other means.[2]

Prayer and Fasting Purifies Us

God does a purifying work in our lives when we fast and pray. Fasting crucifies the flesh so that the Spirit of God can move more freely in our lives. When we determine to fast, then we are determining to remove the obstacles in our life that hinder our relationship with God. On the next page, notice the deep work God does in our life when we spend time in fasting. Carefully meditate on the profound work God does in our heart and soul.

- **Fasting humbles the soul.** God brings us into a deeper level of humility when we fast.

  Yet when they were ill, I put on sackcloth and humbled myself with fasting (Psalm 35:13).

- **Fasting chastens the soul.** The closer we draw to God's heart, the more we will share His sorrows.

  When I weep and fast, I must endure scorn... But I pray to you, LORD, in the time of your favor; in your great love, O God, answer me with your sure salvation (Psalm 69:10, 13).

- **Fasting causes us to sacrifice our personal will.** It is a discipline of the heart, mind, and will.

  I desire to do your will, my God; your law is within my heart (Psalm 40:8).

- **Fasting brings the body into subjection.** We must with rigor serve the Lord and battle against sin.

  Therefore I do not run like a man running aimlessly; I do not fight like a boxer beating the air. No, I strike a blow to my body and make it my slave so that after I have preached to others, I myself will not be disqualified for the prize (1 Corinthians 9:26-27).

- **Fasting breaks down the barriers in man's carnal nature that hinder the Holy Spirit's power.** As a result, the Holy Spirit can work more powerfully through your prayers.

  Now to him who is able to do immeasurably more than all we ask or imagine, according to his power that is at work within us, to him be glory in the church and in Christ Jesus throughout all generations, for ever and ever! Amen (Ephesians 3:20-21).

- **Fasting brings us into a deeper level of brokenness.** We become more dependent on Him and more broken before Him when we go without food.

  My sacrifice, O God, is a broken spirit; a broken and contrite heart you, God, will not despise (Psalm 51:17).

- **Fasting is a time of examination and enables God to focus on our heart.** God examines our inner attitudes and motivation. He is better able to get our attention. Fasting and prayer quiets us so we can more clearly hear His voice.

  Search me, God, and know my heart; test me and know my anxious thoughts. See if there is any offensive way in me, and lead me in the way everlasting (Psalm 139:23-24).

- **Fasting causes us to face ourselves without the normal escape routes.** It brings us into a deeper relationship with God.

  As the deer pants for streams of water, so my soul pants for you, my God. My soul thirsts for God, for the living God (Psalm 42:1-2a).

God desires that we seek a love relationship with Him. He longs for our intimacy. Fasting and prayer removes the distractions from our lives so that we can focus on Him alone. Our relationship becomes purer, and our devotion becomes more intense. We get to the place where we seek God only and not other things. Let the following testimony from Alice Smith speak to your heart. She is an intercessor, author, and leader of the U.S. Prayer Center together with her husband. In her book, *Beyond the Veil*, she says:

> In time, the discerning Bride safe in the arms of her Bridegroom will see "that look in His eye" that communicates lovingly, "Okay beloved, what do you want from Me?" For years I took this opportunity to share my request with Him. Then one day, captivated by His grace and mercy, there seemed only one correct answer, "My beloved Lord, I want only you." Instantly, in the unseen realm, the shouts of joy were heard in heaven as a new breakthrough occurred in the relationship between Jesus and His intercessor. I had been given the opportunity to ask for anything, instead I chose to have more of God. I rejoice in that decision daily. Amazingly, this new victory also ushers in new authority! Unaware of the promotion in heaven's court, the believer who makes this choice waits for a response from the Lord. Imagine His delight with this choice as He answers, "Beloved, I give you more of Me." A metamorphosis occurs as the old nature falls off and the spirit is given new life beyond the veil with Him. True love has taken root.[3]

God will flow through those who intimately know Him.

When we fast and pray we are more sensitive to His presence and more fully yielded to His spirit in humility. God will always use those who are broken and humble in heart. When our carnal nature of selfishness is broken, pride is replaced by submission, and we grow in loving obedience.

We read in James 4:6: *But he gives us more grace. That is why Scripture says: "God opposes the proud, but shows favor to the humble."* When we fast and pray God changes us, and we experience His grace and favor in a greater dimension in our lives.

> The purpose of fasting is not to persuade God. Neither prayer nor fasting is the ultimate tool by which we get God to bless our efforts. We don't wrestle a reluctant God into doing things by denying ourselves as the heathen attempt to do. We serve an omniscient, omnipresent, omnipotent and sovereign God who does all things well. Fasting isn't about changing Him—it is about changing ourselves.[4] Eddie and Alice Smith, *Drawing Closer to God's Heart*

Fasting in Scripture

> Jesus' disciples were perplexed with their lack of spiritual power against darkness. When they asked Jesus why, He explained that this was a situation where prayer with fasting was required. In other words, fasting would empower their prayer and increase their anointing against the forces of evil (Matthew 17:21).[5] Eddie and Alice Smith, *Drawing Closer to God's Heart*

Fasting impacts our life. It is an important discipline for it enables God to lead us deeper into a lifestyle that increases our spiritual authority against the powers of darkness. May God motivate us to seek Him wholeheartedly in fasting and prayer so that we are brought higher into God's ways and plans here on earth.

There are some breakthroughs that will only happen when fasting is combined with prayer.

Some people think that fasting has little value, but the Bible says that some things will not happen without it (Matthew 17:21). We need the power of God in our lives to overcome the powers of darkness.

I read a story about a simple woman in Africa who saw God do many miracles because of prayer and fasting. She had no college degree, but she knew the power of God. When she prayed for the sick, people were healed. Some missionaries saw the power of God displayed through her life and wanted to bring her to Europe and the United States to use her gift to raise money. But when she came, she no longer saw the miracles. The simple reason was that she had quit praying and fasting.

We need to practice the discipline of fasting in order to see the power of God displayed in our life.

There are several kinds of fasts that we can undertake for various reasons. We may enter a fast for personal spiritual growth or for the salvation of family members. There may be an area where we need a breakthrough personally or in our ministry. Keep in mind that fasting should be part of every Christian's life as indicated in Scripture. The Bible speaks much about prayer and fasting. James Packer in his book, *Your Father Loves You,* emphasizes the purposes of fasting:

> In Scripture we see several purposes for fasting. It's part of the discipline of self-control; it's a way of sharing that we depend on God alone and draw all our strength and resources from him; it's a way of focusing totally on him when seeking his guidance and help, and of showing that you really are in earnest in your quest; it's also, at times, an expression of sorrow and deep repentance, something that a person or community will do in order to acknowledge failure before God and seek his mercy.[6]

Various Fasts in Scripture

Elmer L. Town's book, *Fasting for Spiritual Breakthrough,* is a guide to nine Biblical fasts. We need to ask God what kind of fast He wants us to enter and how long He wants us to fast. Here are some examples of fasting in Scripture adapted from his book.[7] Study these carefully, and pray regarding the practice of fasting in your own life. After each fast mentioned, I am including a benefit of fasting found in the fasting chapter in the Bible, Isaiah 58.

- **Jesus' Fast.** At times we may want to fast for spiritual empowerment to do God's will. Jesus spent forty days fasting in the wilderness (Matthew 4:1-11). He was led into the wilderness by the Holy Spirit and came out in the power of the Spirit. Although He was tempted by Satan His life was one that overcame the works of the devil, set the oppressed free, and brought salvation to the world. His life after this fast was one of signs, wonders, and daily miracles.

    ...to loose the chains of injustice and untie the cords of the yoke, to set the oppressed free and break every yoke? (Isaiah 58:6b).

- **The Esther Fast.** Fasting is extremely helpful for protection from the evil one. When we fast for protection and deliverance from Satan, God delivers us from evil and from the works of the enemy. To save her people, the Jews, she called them all to fast for three days and nights with her (Esther 4:16). God honored their fast and protected them from the enemy in a miraculous way.

    ...then your righteousness will go before you, and the glory of the LORD will be your rear guard (Isaiah 58:8b).

- **The Daniel Fast.** There are times when we may want to fast for health and physical healing. Fasting is healthy when done properly, and God will touch our bodies and strengthen us. Daniel ate only vegetables and water with his fast (Daniel 1:12). See Daniel 1:12-20 to find out the effectiveness of his fast. They were stronger than everyone else. They looked better nourished than all the other young men (Daniel 1:15). They were ten times brighter in wisdom and understanding than all the magicians.

    ...and will strengthen your frame. You will be like a well-watered garden, like a spring whose waters never fail (Isaiah 58:11b).

- **The John the Baptist Fast.** A lifestyle that includes fasting will greatly influence others toward repentance and holiness. Fasting before the Lord can help release God's restoration and repair into people's lives. John the Baptist had a lifestyle of fasting, and God used him to lead others into repentance and restoration. He was great in the sight of the Lord and filled with the Holy Spirit (Luke 1:15). His food was locusts and wild honey (Matthew 3:4).

Your people will rebuild the ancient ruins and will raise up the age-old foundations; you will be called Repairer of Broken Walls, Restorer of Streets with Dwellings (Isaiah 58:12).

- **The Elijah Fast.** We may want to fast to defeat some negative emotional or personal habit. Fasting helps us break personal fears and other mental problems. Through fasting God will help us overcome problems such as depression, hopelessness, or discouragement. Elijah was depressed and discouraged, but after eating he was strengthened in spirit physically and emotionally and traveled for forty days and nights (1 Kings 19:2-18). His light broke forth.

Then your light will break forth like the dawn, and your healing will quickly appear (Isaiah 58:8a).

- **The Widow's Fast.** God may want us to fast and provide for the needy. When we put aside our own physical needs, we find that God provides for our needs as He enables us to provide for the needs of others. The widow at Zarephath fed Elijah all that she had. As a result her jar of flour was not used up, and the jug of oil did not run dry (1 Kings 17:12, 15-16).

Is it not to share your food with the hungry and to provide the poor wanderer with shelter—when you see the naked, to clothe them, and not to turn away from your own flesh and blood? Then your light will break forth like the dawn... (Isaiah 58:7-8a).

- **The Apostle Paul's Fast.** At times we may need fasting for insight and guidance. On the Damascus road, Jesus met Paul dramatically. To bring deep focus on the meaning of this encounter, for three days Paul was without the distractions of food, drink, or natural sight (Acts 9:9). If we fast to find out God's will and wisdom, He will reveal it to us.

...then your light will rise in the darkness, and your night will become like the noonday. The LORD will guide you always (Isaiah 58:10b-11a).

Spirit-led prayer and fasting can break the chains and burdens in the lives of others. We have the power of the Holy Spirit available to us. Through prayer, we can destroy the works of the enemy in the lives of those imprisoned by him. Did you know that the New Testament says over forty times that God is the source of our power? We read in John 8:36: *So if the Son sets you free, you will be free indeed.* We must learn to stand strong in God's power (Ephesians 6:10-11).

The fast chosen by the Lord is able to set the captives free as stated in Isaiah 58:6. We can loose the bonds of wickedness and chains of injustice in the lives of others. "To loose" actually means to untie the knot in a rope and to set free. The wicked one has bound many, and we can untie the knot through intercession and bring freedom from bondage for individuals, marriages, families, cities, and nations through prayer and fasting. When someone is yoked, he is forced to serve the enemy. Fasting and prayer can break this yoke, releasing individuals from their prison and shame.

As we grow in prayer, let us practice regular fasting in our personal lives. Let's make sure the discipline of fasting is part of the training for our church and the Christian community in our city.

> Prayer intercession is empowered not only by the Holy Spirit, but also by true Biblical fasting. With revival sweeping the nations, we are hearing of more prayer with fasting than prayer without fasting. We must return to the early church discipline of fasting. This discipline will be part of our training for the Church, especially in the coming generations.[8] Frank Damazio, *Seasons of Intercession*

Fasting the Right Way

And the first thoughts suggested by Jesus' words in regards to fasting and prayer is, that is only in a life of moderation and temperance and self-denial that there will be the heart or the strength to pray much... We are creatures of the senses: our mind is helped by what comes to us embodied in concrete form; fasting helps to express, to deepen, and to confirm the resolution that we are ready to sacrifice anything, to sacrifice ourselves, to attain what we seek for the Kingdom of God.[9] Andrew Murray, *With Christ in the School of Prayer*

Did you know that the famous revivalist, Charles Finney, was a man who prayed and fasted often during his life? I'm sure this was one of the secrets to his amazing fruitfulness. May we be encouraged by his powerful life and testimony. He said:

> I used to spend a great deal of time in prayer; sometimes, I thought, literally praying "without ceasing". I also found it very profitable, and felt very much inclined to hold frequent days of private fasting. On those days I would seek to be entirely alone with God, and would generally wander off into the woods, or get into the meeting house, or somewhere away entirely by myself. But whenever I fasted, and let the Spirit take his own course with me, and gave myself up to let him lead and instruct me, I universally found it in the highest degree useful. I found I could not live without enjoying the presence of God.[10]

As we enter into fasting—whether it is a meal, a day, or a season of fasting—let us make sure that we are fasting the right way. Let us ask God for the right heart motives and enter into our fast with a humble and obedient heart. Wrong fasting accomplishes nothing. It's an outward act of religious obedience, but it has no heart. It can be a ritualistic duty that causes pride and self-importance.

Wrong fasting does not satisfy the heart of God. He is looking for those who draw near to Him with humility of heart, honesty, and submission. We must have clean hearts. He is looking for the right heart attitude and motives. This is why some do not see spiritual breakthroughs in their lives. We see this in Isaiah 58:3-5, where the people continued to live disobedient and rebellious lives against God's moral laws even though they were fasting.

> *'Why have we fasted', they say, 'and you have not seen it? Why have we humbled ourselves, and you have not noticed?' "Yet on the day of your fasting, you do as you please and exploit all your workers. Your fasting ends in quarreling and strife, and in striking each other with wicked fists. You cannot fast as you do today and expect your voice to be heard on high. Is this the kind of fast*

I have chosen, only a day for people to humble themselves? Is it only for bowing one's head like a reed and for lying in sackcloth and ashes? Is that what you call a fast, a day acceptable to the LORD?

The right kind of fasting is very beneficial. God rewards fasting that is done the right way. He looks at our hearts. If we fast the way God desires, with an attitude of humility, He will bring rich blessings. Right fasting sees results.

Isaiah 58 speaks at great length about the numerous benefits of fasting with the right heart. We've seen how the Biblical examples of fasting produced many of these benefits. This chapter alone should motivate us to seek God more diligently in prayer and fasting. The benefits of right fasting are found in Isaiah 58:5-12:

- Your light will break forth like the dawn (verse 8).

- Your healing will quickly appear (verse 8).

- Your righteousness will go before you (verse 8).

- The glory of the Lord will be your rear guard (verse 8).

- You will call and the Lord will answer (verse 9).

- You will cry for help, and he will say, "Here am I" (verse 9).

- Your light will arise in the darkness (verse 10).

- Your night will become like the noonday (verse 10).

- The Lord will guide you always (verse 11).

- The Lord will satisfy your needs in a sun-scorched land (verse 11).

- The Lord will strengthen your frame (verse 11).

- You will be like a well-watered garden, like a spring whose waters never fail (verse 11).

- Your people will rebuild the ancient ruins and will raise up the age-old foundations (verse 12).

- You will be called repairer of broken walls (verse 12).

- You will be a restorer of streets with dwellings (verse 12).

- You will find your joy in the Lord (verse 14).

- You will rise on the heights of the land (verse 14).

- You will feast on the inheritance of your father Jacob (verse 14).

We all want to see the power of God in our lives and ministry. We want to see the lost saved and the sick healed. We want to pray and stand in the gap for others. Then we must introduce fasting into our lifestyle. The hour is urgent. God is looking for those who will have a lifestyle of fasting and prayer.

Wherever you are now in your life regarding this most important discipline, pray and ask Him to bring you further. He will help you to incorporate this into your life so that you will rise on the heights of the land. Let's move forward together in prayer and fasting so that we will have powerful Kingdom results in our lives.

> Prayer intercession moves into the breach, the spiritual gap, and begins to pray repentance, restoration, revival and redirection for people—saved and unsaved. This should be the intercessor's prayer while fasting. This is the prayer God desires from fasting intercessors. "Is this not the fast that I have chosen?" Combine this spirit of intercession with the fasting of an honest heart, with Isaiah 58:6-12 to guide us, and the result will be powerful prayers with Kingdom results.[11] Frank Damazio, *Seasons of Intercession*

Deeper Still Life Application
How to Practice Personal Fasting

We've looked at the purifying power of prayer and fasting, what the Scriptures say about fasting, and fasting the right way. Spend adequate time going through this chapter, asking God how He wants you to apply it into your life. Carefully study the various fasts in Scripture, choose one of these fasts, and pick a date to fast. Keep the following in mind:

- Prepare your heart and your body for a fast - You may want to cut back on food and coffee before your fast. Drink plenty of water during your fast.

- Ask God to give you some key things to pray for during your fast - Spend some time in interceding for others.

- Spend a lot of time in worship and thanksgiving - Keep your mind on God and His attributes.

- Concentrate on the Word of God - Study Isaiah 58, especially the benefits of fasting in verses 5-12.

- Examine your heart - Repent of your sins and shortcomings.

- Present your needs before God - Tell Him the needs and concerns in your heart, the difficulties you face, and what you desire for Him to do for you.

- Journal during your fast - Write down anything He tells you and any insight He give you during your fast.

- Read books on fasting - You may want to read a book on fasting before or during a fast. See www.intercessorsarise.org for a list of key books on fasting and prayer.

How to Help Others Practice Personal Fasting

Get together with an individual or group, and study this chapter together. Carefully study the various fasts in Scripture, choose one of these fasts, and pick a date to fast together as a group. During your fast, practice the points listed in the life application.

After your fast is over, meet together as a group and discuss any insights God has given you. Talk about what you learned personally and as a group during your fast. Discuss how you will go deeper in a fasting lifestyle. End with praying as a group the following prayer. You may want to consider fasting again together as a group in the future.

My Prayer to God

Lord, I want to grow in my ability to fast and pray. Enable me to bring my body into subjection through fasting. I do not want to fast aimlessly (1 Corinthians 9:26-27). Help me to incorporate fasting into my lifestyle on a regular basis. I want your Spirit to work more powerfully through my prayers. Help me to fast the right way as Your Word says in Isaiah 58:5-12. Examine my inner attitudes and motivation. "Search me, God, and know my heart; test me and know my anxious thoughts. See if there is any offensive way in me, and lead me in the way everlasting" (Psalm 139:23-24).

Purify my heart, and bring me into a deeper relationship with You. Remove every distraction from my life. I want a love relationship with You. Break the chains and burdens in my life and the chains of injustice in my nation. I want to draw closer to Your throne and move higher in my commitment to Your purposes. Through fasting, help me to stand in the gap for others in intercession. I want to see the lost saved and the sick healed through my prayers. Give me a hunger for Your presence, and help me to grow in a fasting lifestyle for Your honor and glory. I thank you for the blessings of fasting in Your Word in Isaiah 58:5-12. [Pray these verses for your life.] "Then your light will break forth like the dawn, and your healing will quickly appear; then your righteous will go before you, and the glory of the LORD will be your rear guard. Then you will call, and the LORD will answer; you will cry for help, and he will say: Here am I"… I pray this in Jesus' name, amen.

CHAPTER NINE

DEEPER IN PASSIONATE FERVENCY

The righteous cry out,
and the LORD hears them;
he delivers them from all their trouble.
Psalm 34:17

ROCKING BACK AND FORTH as he prays, he has attracted multitudes of young people because of his fervent and committed lifestyle. Many may look on and say, "This is a modern day John the Baptist." Others have been challenged by his strong and steadfast commitment to fervent prayer and fasting. He is a man who is passionate in prayer.

Lou Engle is internationally known as the leader of TheCall. He is best known among the youth for organizing solemn assemblies of fasting and prayer, especially for asking God in prayer to stop abortion and bring justice to America.

Norm and I had the privilege of attending the first one in America several years ago right on the mall of the Capital. These prayer meetings are known for not seeking to entertain people but to encounter God. The best way I can describe that day of prayer and fasting was passionate prayer. Led and organized by Lou Engle, these are passionate solemn assemblies of fasting and prayer attended by thousands—especially young people—and the assemblies continue and the fervency increases.

Let me tell you a little about Lou. His journey in prayer began much earlier. He was a man who cultivated passionate prayer in the secret place when he was young. When I think of His name, I think of the word "fervent" or "passionate" because this is exactly what he is. He cries out to God to bring justice onto the earth and to stop abortion and sin. He knows what it means to be desperate for God and passionate for revival. I know this is true because he is based at the International House of Prayer here in Kansas City where I am on staff. I see his life in the Global Prayer Room whenever he is in town.

Passionate fervency is characteristic of his prayer life.

Lou is an eighth generation descendent of Jacob Engle. Fleeing from religious persecution in Switzerland in the 1700's, Jacob's family fled to the United States. Jacob was the only child to survive crossing the Atlantic. Because of this, mothers on board wondered at the greatness of his destiny. Generations later Lou—a man of destiny—made a covenant before God to seek revival regardless of the cost like in Acts 2. He left seminary and took a job mowing lawns and spent hours in prayer daily asking God to send revival.

He was greatly impacted by the Promise Keepers, where one million men were ignited with a passion for Jesus and to a lifestyle of purity and godliness. He had a God-given dream to raise-up a youth movement to cry out to God for a revival to sweep across America.

Two years after this vision, a woman approached him and asked if he ever considered putting young people on the Mall like the Promise Keepers. He told her how he was greatly burdened with a dream to see youth gathered at the National Mall. He felt that this gathering would be a sign from God that there was hope for America. That woman promptly wrote a check for $100,000 that resulted in TheCall DC on September 2, 2000. Over 400 thousand young people attended TheCall DC. It was an amazing time of prayer, worship, repentance, and encouragement from our nation's spiritual leaders. I can testify that the presence of God was strongly present during that day.

Now looking back on this one man's life, we see that his fervent prayers have led to multitudes of radical young people seeking revival through prayer and fasting all across the nations. Even at the time of this writing, Lou was getting ready to start another forty-day fast. He prepares the way for the Lord through his passionate prayer for revival and his upright lifestyle. Like John the Baptist, Luke 3:4-6 is characteristic of Lou's job description:

As is written in the book of the words of Isaiah the prophet: "A voice of one calling in the wilderness, 'Prepare the way for the Lord, make straight paths for him. Every valley shall be filled in, every mountain and hill made low. The crooked roads shall become straight, the rough ways smooth. And all people will see God's salvation.'"

All of us are called to prepare the way for the coming of the Lord. In these last two chapters, we will not only look at going deeper personally, but we will see how God wants to bring city transformation and revival through our prayers. God wants to take us deeper in passionate fervency.

You may desire to have a more fervent prayer life and wonder, "How can I be passionate in prayer like Lou Engle? How can I learn to pray powerful prayers that bring transformation to my family, city, or nation?" In this chapter let's learn about the power of crying out to God. Discover how to have passion for revival, and find out why desperation is the key to transformation—not only in your life but also in the life of your city.

The Power of Crying Out

In moments of fear, anxiety, and trouble, the right step toward experiencing God's powerful deliverance and protection is to simply cry out—to use our voice in fervent appeal for His help.[1]
Bill Gothard, *The Power of Crying Out*

Do you ever practice crying out loud to God for help?

I think most of us have, especially when we've been in serious trouble. This is how our Biblical predecessors often prayed. Fervency in prayer and crying out loud is a key to breakthrough in prayer. Norm has often told people that fervent, passionate prayer is the type of prayer you would cry out if your airplane were falling from the sky. You would cry out to God in desperation, with all of your heart! There would be no place for distracted, apathetic prayer under those circumstances. No way! It would be a life and death matter.

Yet many of us are facing impossible circumstances where the "crying out" type of prayer is needed for spiritual breakthrough. Crying out loud seems to be a key to a powerful prayer life that influences heaven and sees tremendous answers to prayer. Often we are urged by the Spirit to cry an impassioned declaration of God's powerful ability. That demonstrates our total dependence on God to accomplish the victory. We need to catch hold of this truth and apply it to our prayer lives. We read in Psalm 86:7: *When I am in distress, I call to you, because you answer me.* When we cry out to God, we experience His all-sufficient, supernatural power to answer us.

God often arranges our circumstances so there seems to be no way out.

Haven't you been there? The problem doesn't seem to go away. But in response to our crying out to Him, He answers. He may bring healing, protection, or direction. He wants to show us that He is our sole saving power when we are at the end of all our known resources. In the Bible, there is a consistent pattern of God's people crying out to Him and His answering in His power. David often cried aloud to God with deep emotion when in desperate situations, and God answered his cry. He says in Psalm 34:17: The *righteous cry out, and the LORD hears them; he delivers them from all their trouble.* Bill Gothard in his book, *The Power of Crying Out,* states:

> Many believers today seem unaware of this consistent pattern in God's Word. It could even be said that the most significant difference between the prayers of God's saints in Scripture (so powerfully effective) and our prayers today (so seemingly ineffective) is this: There was a fervency in the prayers of Biblical saints—a fervency that is inherent in crying out.[2]

Crying out to God is not something we do mechanically, but it flows out of our relationship with Him. Do we really know that God actually hears us and longs to hear our cry? He is our Father and loves to hear our voice. We have the authority and right as His children to call fervently to our Father. Do we realize that there is power in the spoken word? When it is spoken fervently, sincerely, and with all our heart, it is even more powerful. Do we realize that as we cry out to God aloud, He sees that we are seriously and boldly coming to His throne of grace? Do we not comprehend that when we cry out to God in our distress He will answer?

We will see that crying out in prayer is the very turning point that brings His deliverance. It happened often in the Bible and can happen for us as well. Notice in Psalm 107:6, 13, 19, and 28 how God loves to answer those with a sincere heart in their need: *Then they cried out to the Lord in their trouble, and He delivered them out of their distresses.* Crying out triggers God's deliverance.

Many of you are facing desperate situations in your life. Learn to cry aloud to God with all your heart. Trust Him—your deliverer—to undertake in your behalf.

> Days of trouble. Hours of crisis. Moments of urgent and fearful need. They come to us all unexpectedly, like a thief in the night. How can we prepare for such times? We can prepare by being ready to cry aloud to the Lord for His saving help, boldly expecting His deliverance. God invites and expects His beloved ones to do exactly that: "Call upon Me in the day of trouble," He tells us; "I will deliver you, and you shall glorify Me."[3] Bill Gothard, *The Power of Crying Out*

As I have already mentioned the Doulos, this ship that sailed from country to country was our home for several years. I've told this story in my book called, *Intercessors Arise,* but I wanted to emphasize it again here because it so distinctly shows us the power of crying out.

During one of our voyages—with over three hundred people from forty nations aboard—we were sailing down the coast of South America and were about to enter the Straits of Magellan. This is a narrow, long passage of quite some distance off the coast of Chile. Our next port of ministry was the southernmost city at the tip of Chile. You could consider this area of the world the "ends of the earth." The straits are known for their treacherous and dangerous seas.

The weather at the time was stormy, and the waves were choppy and unsafe. This would make it very difficult for our old ship to pass through safely. This ship—built in 1914 and in the Guinness Book of World Records as the oldest floating passenger ship in the world—caused many of us even more concern as we anticipated this dangerous journey.

In light of our situation, the captain made an urgent request over the loud speaker. He said that we must all gather together immediately and pray for God to calm the seas. We must cry out to God to give us safe passage through the Straits of Magellan so that we could arrive on time at our next port.

With no time to waste, the entire staff and crew gathered together in our main lounge to pray. Imagine the thoughts that raced through our minds and the level of anxiety many of us felt as we hurried to the main lounge. After all, we were on a tiny, old ship anticipating tossing around in treacherous seas. We felt dependent at that moment on a supernatural God who could turn our situation around by His power and might.

We began to pray and cry out to God to calm the seas for His glory. Perhaps you can guess what happened next. Yes! God answered prayer—the seas became still—and the ship passed peacefully through the narrow passage.

My future husband and I sat on deck and admired the beauty of God's creation in this gorgeous part of the world. We had met each other on board, and this was our first date and one we will always remember. During that voyage we saw many shipwrecks along the way—right in the midst of all the natural beauty of massive rocks and clear blue seas. This was a vivid reminder of God's powerful answer to our desperate prayers.

Is crying out to God effective?

It certainly is. Our ship was able to reach its destination safely. We were able to continue our conferences and evangelistic programs right on schedule. God used such a situation to build our faith as we cried out to Him and lived His answer. He wants to break through in extreme situations. He will do the same for you as He did for us on this voyage. I recommend that you read and pray through some of the heartfelt prayers of David. Psalms 16, 25, 31, 51, and 63 are excellent Psalms that you can pray out loud for yourself and others.

You may be passing through dangerous or difficult waters. God wants you to know that He hears your cry. He wants to take you deeper in passionate, fervent prayer. And remember when He answers your prayers, be sure to give thanks to Him for His unfailing love and His wonderful deeds on your behalf. Crying out to God for help is a wonderful way to live. We not only should do it during times of trouble but as we pray for revival in our city and nation. God loves it when we pray with fervency and passion.

> *Then they cried out to the LORD in their trouble, and he brought them out of their distress. He stilled the storm to a whisper; the waves of the sea were hushed. They were glad when it grew calm, and he guided them to their desired haven. Let them give thanks to the LORD for his unfailing love and his wonderful deeds for mankind (Psalm 107:28-31).*

Revival Passion

Every significant outpouring of the Spirit seems to have been preceded by earnest, agonizing intercession, accompanied by a heartbrokenness and humiliation before God... Let no one pray for revival—let no one pray for a mighty baptism of power who is not prepared for deep heart-searchings and confession of sin in his personal life. Revival, in its beginnings, is a most humiliating experience. When one, like Isaiah, sees himself in the light of God's holiness he must inevitably cry, "Woe is me!" Deep spiritual awakenings, whether in local churches or in whole countries, begin with desperate people.[4] Rick Joyner, "Lessons on the Welsh Revival"

There has never been a revival without passion.

Revival passion is key to a deeper prayer life. We just saw how God answers us when we passionately cry out to Him. But did you know that the intense level of intercession before revival is extraordinary as well? There is a deep heart-searching and desperation over personal sin and the sin of the people. The Welsh revival had these characteristics— a deep conviction of sin along with intercession and repentance. Many of us find it very hard to add prayer meetings into our already busy schedules, but when a mighty revival is moving, all of this doesn't seem to matter. Prayer and getting right with God become all important.

In pondering such moves of God and seeing our need for passionate prayer and a greater concern for souls, certainly our desperate cry should be for revival to sweep across the nations. We need to search our own hearts and cry out, "God, purify me!" Evan Roberts, the young man who was used so powerfully by God in the Welsh revival of 1904, prayed passionately that God would purify and bend the Church. He prayed that God would break his own heart over the condition of mankind. His heart was set on obedience. Agonizing prayer was his daily lifestyle. Well-known author and founder of Morningstar, Rick Joyner, said this about him:

> Evan Roberts captured the spirit of the whole revival with the theme: Bend the Church and Save the World. James E. Stewart claimed that this is the secret of every true awakening. Christians must humble themselves and get right with God so that the Spirit can break through in converting power upon the unsaved. There must be no hypocrisy; the Christian must bend to all the will of God for His life in perfect obedience before the Spirit of God is released. When we are bent to the will of God we will be intercessors, because as He "ever lives to intercede" for His people, if we are abiding in Him we will do the same.[5]

Are we willing to pay the price to actually let God bend and purify us as he did Evan Roberts?

Characteristics of Revival Passion

It is helpful to look at some of the meanings of the word "passion" in Webster's Dictionary as we think of the characteristics of revival passion. The word "passion" means: "highly excited, expressing strong emotion, with strong feeling, zeal, eager desire."[6] Great passion and zeal were expressed in the past revivals. This passion was for holiness, for purity of life, and for obedience.

Those in the revival had strong emotions as they yearned for the salvation of the lost. Because of their great passion for souls, preachers were zealous for a fearless proclamation of the truth and brought God's word with deep conviction and mighty unction, bringing sinners face to face with the Almighty God. As a result, multitudes would weep with great agony of soul as they were confronted with the sin in their own heart. These were the characteristics of revivals in the past. This is what we need in our present day.

- **A passion for God's Word and anointed preaching.** Revivals are characterized by a powerful and passionate proclamation of the truth. The preaching is extremely anointed, spontaneous, and fearless. Revival preaching centers on Christ, bringing conviction of sin to all its listeners. The words are spoken with a demonstration of the power of God with a supernatural boldness and unction. People are hungry for God's Word.

In the Evans Mills revival, Finney recalls: "The Spirit of God came upon me with such power that it was like opening a battery upon them. For more than an hour, the Word of God came through me to them in such a manner that I could see was carrying all before it. It was a fire and a hammer breaking the rock, and as the word that was piercing... I saw a general conviction was spreading over the whole audience."[7] Winkie Pratney, "The Nature of Revival"

My message and my preaching were not with wise and persuasive words, but with a demonstration of the Spirit's power (1 Cor. 2:4).

- **A passion for prayer and holiness.** Those in the revival had a deep passion for prayer and for getting their lives right with God. There was no toleration of sin. There was humility, an urgent confession of sin, and a holy fear of God. Worldliness was forsaken and large numbers would attend early prayer meetings on a daily basis. People were bent on obeying the will of God.

Thousands of believers, often unknown to each other, in small towns and great cities, cried to God day after day for the fire of revival to fall. This was not merely "a little talk with Jesus" but daily agonizing intercession. These were devoted saints who had given their lives to the sacrifice of prayer and worship. They were so jealous for the name of their God that they agonized day and night because of the way Satan was being glorified all around them and they yearned from the depths of their beings to see the Lord's name lifted up in Wales. They constantly reminded God of what He had done in 1859, through the Second Great Awakening, and begged Him to pour out His Spirit again.[8] Rick Joyner, "Lessons on the Welsh Revival"

Create in me a pure heart, O God, and renew a steadfast spirit within me (Psalm 51:10).

- **A Passion for the Lost.** The concern for the lost during the revival was extraordinary. There was praying with tears and a passion to see souls saved. The joy of knowing Christ could not be hidden. Everyone was a brightly shining lamplight to neighbors and co-workers, powerfully attracting unbelievers to that light.

  There can be no revival without soul-winning. In saving lost souls the Welsh Revival must be considered one of the most intense and effective revivals of all time. This was not a program for a few preachers or a campaign to get church members testifying to the saving grace of the Lord Jesus. There were no classes given on how to reach the lost. It just seemed that every Christian in Wales erupted simultaneously with a burning agony for the lost. The joy of salvation simply could not be contained by the believers as every coal mine, tramcar, office, school or ship became a pulpit for the gospel... There was no set pattern of strategy for the witnessing; it was simply born out of an overflowing joy and faith that could not be contained in those who knew the Savior.[9] Rick Joyner, "The Welsh Revival"

  Those who accepted his message were baptized, and about three thousand souls were added to their number that day (Acts 2:41).

Fervent, passionate prayer for revival in our churches will change the messages in the pulpit into ones of tremendous power.

Five young college students were spending a Sunday in London, and they decided to go and hear the well-known preacher, Charles Spurgeon. While they were waiting for the doors of the church to open, a man greeted them at the door and asked, "Gentlemen, would you like me to show you around the church? Would you like me to show you the heating plant of this church?" It was a very hot day in July and so they were not very excited about his offer. But they said, "Yes" because they didn't want to offend the man. The young men were taken down a long stairway, and the door was quietly opened. Their guide whispered to them, "This is our heating plant." The young college students looked through the door in complete surprise.

In that room were seven hundred people bowed in passionate prayer seeking God's blessing on the service that would soon begin in the auditorium above. The guide softly closed the door. He turned to them and introduced himself as Charles Spurgeon.[10]

Passionate prayer was the secret to his powerful preaching.

Passionate and desperate prayer will be characteristic of the coming revival. God wants to take us deeper in passion and fervency in our prayers. As we continue looking at the importance of this quality of prayer, let's look at what it means to be desperate in prayer. Holy desperation for the presence of God is the key to transformation. Are we desperate enough to change our lifestyles for God?

> Both international and local revivals have been distinctly linked to special prayer... The coming revival will be no exception. An extraordinary spirit of prayer, urging believers to much secret and united prayer, pressing them to labor fervently (Col. 4:12) in their supplications, will be one of the surest signs of approaching showers and floods of blessing.[11] Andrew Murray, *Andrew Murray on Prayer*

Holy Desperation

The key of holy desperation for the presence and ministry of Jesus is required in order for us to move out of our complacent, satisfied existence. Desperation is the underlying fuel that ignites our hearts for unity, prayer, worship, and repentance. If we aren't longing for Jesus our ministry activities will be routine and hollow. There is certainly no shortage of ideas, plans, methods, books, teachings, programs, and activities in the church; what we are suffering from is a drought of desperation for God![12] Rhonda Hughey, *Desperate for His Presence*

Are we desperate enough for God? Are we each willing to pay the price that desperation requires of us in our lives?

I taste the level of commitment necessary for city transformation whenever I am involved in a 24/7 House of Prayer. I remember how I felt after finishing a one-month House of Prayer in Spain. It had radically changed my life, just as it did with others who had stepped into the fire of God's presence in that location in southern Spain. Prayer lives had been challenged. The question I had to ask myself was:

- How far am I willing to go?
- How desperate am I willing to become?
- Can I even begin to think about going back to how things were before?

The answer was, "No." It was time to proceed. Many of us had stepped in this far and the levels of commitment required were going higher. God had challenged us to a new phase, a new mountain to climb for His glory. He wanted us to go deeper in holy desperation. The battle had been great, and there was no turning back.

There was something so exceeding real and alive to that dimension of living.

There was something so necessary and dynamic to that taste of unity between the churches. Suddenly, we realized that we were in this together, and we desperately needed one another to touch that region of Spain with God's glory. I began to value and love the body of Christ in all its' dimensions as I had never done before. I began to understand what it meant to be members of one another. We had tapped into God's wonderful plan for Kingdom living, and I never wanted to return to the old ways.

God had brought me a step further in holy desperation during that time. I felt really alive with the purposes of God for that region of the world.

We will not see transformation in our cities and neighborhoods until our hearts move into a greater level of holy desperation for God. Rhonda Hughey in her book, *Desperate for His Presence*, shares about purposely pursuing God. She says:

> The decision to make a radical lifestyle change and realign our hearts with the Lord is a matter of our will availing itself of God's grace and reprioritizing our time and commitments. We can willingly and purposely begin to pursue God! When we do, He responds, and the more time we spend in His presence, the more desperate for Him we will become. It's an interesting dynamic; the hungrier we are for Him, the hungrier we will become for more of Him![13]

There are ways we can evaluate our cities and our personal lives to see if they are on their way towards transformation. There are several ways to discern if the signs of transformation are present and increasing in our city. George Otis, Jr. gives several indicators of transformation. Below are some indicators adapted from his study.[14] Take time to regularly evaluate your city and your personal life, and pray through these indicators. Most of our cities have a long way to go, but desperate prayer and revival passion is the key. Study and pray these verses over the area where you live as well. Take inventory and prayerfully answer these questions about your own life regarding holy desperation.

- **The political leaders acknowledge their sin and dependence on God.** Jonah 3:6-9 and 2 Kings 11:17-18; 23:2.

  Do I acknowledge sin in my own life? In what areas do I need to grow in holiness? Make a list.

- **The economic conditions improve.** Psalm 144:14; 2 Chronicles 17:3-5; Isaiah 60:5; and Amos 9:13.

  Am I wise in my spending, and do I give to the Lord's work? Am I an extravagant and cheerful giver?

- **Kingdom values are integrated into daily life.** Ezra 10:4; Nehemiah 8:10; Ecclesiastes 10:17; and Acts 19:17-20.

  Am I practicing Kingdom living in my own life? See the Sermon on the Mount in Matthew 5-7.

- **Crime and corruption diminish.** Nehemiah 5:6-12; 2 Kings 12:13-15; and Isaiah 60:17-18.

  Are there any evil practices in the way I live?

- **New laws are put into effect.** Nehemiah 10:31 and 2 Chronicles 19:10.

  Am I obedient to the laws of God? Where do I need to grow in obeying God's Word?

- **The natural environment is restored.** Leviticus 26:4-5; 2 Chronicles 7:14; Ezekiel 34:27; and 36:29-30.

How am I helping, or hindering, God's natural environment? Do I pick up trash outdoors?

- **There is a decline in divorce, bankruptcy, and suicide.** Nehemiah 12:27-28, 43; Isaiah 54:11-14; 62:3, 7; Jer. 30:17-22; 31:11-13; and Hosea 2:15.

  How are my family relationships? In what way am I seeking to help those who are struggling with marriage, hopelessness, or poverty?

- **Christians take responsibility in healing and helping their community.** Isaiah 58:10-12 and 61:104.

  In what ways am I helping my community? Do I pray for my neighbourhood on a regular basis?

- **Christians take revival into other cities and countries.** Isaiah 61:6; 2 Chronicles 17:9; and Acts 11:20-26.

  What is the level of my revival passion? Am I fervent for revival in my city and nation, or am I apathetic?

We will not begin to see this kind of transformation in our cities unless we first become desperate for God. He wants us to become so desperate for His presence that we want it more than anything else in the world. What does desperation look like? Let me give you a good example.

A young man approached the Greek philosopher Socrates and said, "O great Socrates, I come to you for knowledge."

Socrates took this young man and walked him down to the sea. They waded into the water, and he dunked the young man under the water for thirty seconds. Finally, he let the man up for air and asked him to repeat what he wanted. He sputtered, "Knowledge, O great one."

So Socrates dunked him under the water and held him there a little longer. He then asked the question again. After several dunkings and responses, the philosopher asked, "What do you want?"

The young man gasped, "Air, I want air!"

"Good," said Socrates, "When you want knowledge as much as you want air, you shall have it."

In a similar way, God wants us to be desperate for His presence like this young man gasping for air. Life is full of challenges. There is not one of us who does not face difficult circumstances at times. Many of us have faced moments of desperation in this life.

- If you've just lost your job and have five children to take care of, you know what it's like to be desperate.

- If you are starving and are searching everywhere for a meal, you know what it's like to be desperate.

- If you've been saved out of drugs, have overcome alcohol, have lost a loved one, or have lived through a terminal disease, you know what it's like to be desperate.

- If you remember what it's like to be lost, searching for the answer, and not know what it's like to have Jesus, you know what it's like to be desperate.

God wants us to seek Him desperately. He invites us to seek Him with all of our heart. He wants to take us *deeper still* in passionate fervency.

Desperation is one of the secrets to a deeper prayer life. Are you willing to respond to this invitation? The door is before you—the door of intimacy and the door to His presence. Let's invite the King of glory to radically come into our lives and take over, asking Him to make us passionate in prayer. He wants us to be desperate for His presence and for the transformation of our city. Nothing will happen without Him.

Let's invite the King of glory in. Let's say like David in Psalm 24:9-10:

> *Lift up your heads, you gates; lift them up, you ancient doors, that the King of glory may come in. Who is he, this King of glory? The LORD Almighty—he is the King of glory.*

"Lord, we open the door to your invitation. Make us holy and righteous. Radically change our personal lives and reprioritize everything. We seek Your face. Make us hungry Lord. Make us desperate for You and Your presence. In Jesus' name, amen."

To be desperate means to be without hope in your current condition and to know that in your own power you don't have the necessary resources required to change it. People who are desperate become determined to find help, often taking great risks to meet their desperate need. In the communities where transforming revival has occurred the people of God were desperate enough to change their lifestyle and their priorities and to commit their time and resources, making everything secondary to the desperate pursuit of God in their midst. They cried out in desperation, and the Lord heard their cry.[15] Rhonda Hughey, *Desperate for His Presence*

Deeper Still Life Application
How to Grow in Passionate Prayer

Think about your life and experiences where you have felt desperate and have cried out to the Lord. Answer the following in light of your experience:

- Read Psalm 61:1; 85:7; and 107:28-31 - Write a paragraph about a time when you cried out to the Lord in a distressing situation where there seemed to be no way out and where God heard, delivered, and guided you to your desired haven. Give thanks for how He helped you then and how he helps you in times of distress and difficulty.

- Pick one of the heartfelt prayers of David in Psalms 16; 25; 31; 51; or 63 - Pray it to the Lord regarding a trial or difficult situation that you may be facing.

- Evaluate your life in the area of passion - How passionate are you for the Word of God, for prayer and holiness, and for reaching the lost? These were the characteristics of revivals in the past. Spend at last ten minutes asking God to make you more passionate in these areas of your life. Ask Him what action or lifestyle change you should make in becoming more passionate for revival. Write down anything He may be saying to you or any action steps He may want you to take. For example, talking to your neighbor about Christ, spending more time daily in prayer or Bible study, praying regularly with your spouse, etc.

- How desperate are you for transformation in your city and personal life? - Look at the indicators for transformation in cities in this chapter. Evaluate your city and pray through these indicators using the Bible in your prayers. Try doing a Bible study on all the verses mentioned in the list. Evaluate your life by answering the personal questions regarding holy desperation.

- Invite the Lord to make you passionate and desperate for His presence - Spend some time in prayer, and end with "My Prayer to God."

How to Help Others
Grow in Passionate Prayer

Get together with an individual or group after first completing the above assignment individually. Open in prayer and begin by reading Psalm 61:1; 85:7; and 107:28-31. Discuss how God has helped each person in distressing situations when they cried out to Him. This can be quite an enlightening discussion as you see how powerfully God answers the cries of His people.

Have each one share about areas in their life where they need to be more passionate for revival. What action steps are they taking? Together evaluate the Christians in your city in the area of desperation. Look at some of the key verses in this chapter. Spend adequate time in prayer, bringing your discussion before the Lord, and praying for a greater desperation for His presence.

This application assignment could be divided into three weekly sessions if you desire more time for a thorough discussion and prayer time. End with praying together "My Prayer to God."

My Prayer to God

Lord, help me to be more passionate in prayer. I want to learn the secret of crying out to You. I want to live a dependent and totally yielded life. Thank you for the impossible situations where you have heard and guided me (Psalm 61:1; 107:28-31). [Name an impossible situation you have faced]. "For you have been my refuge, a strong tower against the foe. I long to dwell in your tent forever and take refuge in the shelter of your wings" (Psalm 61:3-4). I thank You that You love to answer me in my need (Psalm 107:6, 13, 19, and 28). I can trust in You for deliverance.

Teach me to passionately cry out to You for revival. Search my heart, and make me desperate for You. Bend me like you did Evan Roberts. Teach me brokenness and humility. Help me to walk low and give You all the glory. Help me to walk in repentance. Make me passionate for holiness, for purity of life, and for obedience. Make me passionate for Your Word. Give me passion for the salvation of the lost.

Bring revival to my life and the life of others in my city. Help the Church in my city to focus on your Kingdom in everything we do. Make us desperate for Your presence. Bring the churches in my city together in unity. Teach us to walk together, and love and esteem one another. Help us to find ways to worship and pray together. Show us our city through Your eyes. Give us a heart for the lost and the broken-hearted in our city. Help us to walk in Your authority and power. Fill our city with a spirit of prayer and intercession. We seek Your face. In Jesus' name, amen.

CHAPTER TEN

DEEPER IN GOD'S PRESENCE

You have made known to me the path of life;
you will fill me with joy in your presence,
with eternal pleasures at your right hand.
Psalm 16:11

COULD GOD POSSIBLY DO ANYTHING in this part of the world now? Could it possibly be true that there was a new expectation and hope in a region where darkness had invaded that area of the world for centuries? Could we ever expect Him to invade the Campo de Gibraltar with His awesome presence?

These were our initial thoughts as we launched out by faith and crossed the ocean on an airplane to Spain. There were numerous obstacles. The church is small. The ground is hard. There is a need for lots of faithful and persistent prayer. Would there be enough prayer warriors to take up such a huge challenge?

But God was in the center of this spiritual adventure, and to our joy and amazement, the churches did begin to come together to pray.

In southern Spain, through persistent prayer, there was a big invitation for God's presence. As I mentioned in the last chapter, there was a one-month, 24/7 House of Prayer. There were heart-felt prayers asking God to come and dwell in that area of Spain, Gibraltar, and North Africa.

There was one prayer meeting after another—sometimes two churches met at the same time; sometimes there was one or two praying in the early morning. At other times there was loud praying and praise—and the room was filled with the fragrance of Christ. God was changing all of our lives in the midst of it all.

One night the pastors in the area spent the whole night in prayer together. There was the sense that prayer had reached a new level, and there was a magnetic attraction to the prayer room. I personally found it quite appealing and couldn't wait to get to the prayer room. There seemed to be an unusual grace to pray long hours where it seemed but a few moments.

The presence of God is needed in every city in every nation. God is looking for those who will give themselves to prayer and to seeking His face. In this book you have learned to go deeper with God in so many ways—strategic prayer, partnering with His Spirit, spiritual insight, and a fasting lifestyle. Now it's time to take your deep walk with God into the world. Prayer warriors are needed to contend for His presence everywhere. God wants to take you deeper into His presence not only personally, but he wants to invade your city and nation with His presence.

Maybe you are thinking, "How can I pursue God's presence in a deeper dimension? What are the things in my life that stop Him from coming into my life and into my city?" Let's discover what the Bible says about God's presence. Let's find out what are the hindrances, and look at the evidence of God's manifest presence when it does invade a city.

Pursuing God's Presence

In every revival in history we read a similar testimony. When God responded to His people by sending His presence, He didn't just work himself into their routine religion—He overtook them by His power and glory! He left a trail of glorious chaos in His wake—weeping, repenting, rejoicing, reconciling, changing of habits, healing of families! Nobody wondered if Jesus was involved in these meetings. There was no doubt in their minds and no lack in their hearts.[1] Rhonda Hughey, *Desperate for His Presence*

The purpose of our life is to pursue God.

It is what we were created to do. God wants us to seek and long passionately for His presence. His presence is real and tangible. It will change our lives completely. The problem is that most of us are not aware of what is available to us. Our hearts are not burning for God, and we have settled for lesser things.

In our month-long House of Prayer, several churches in the area of southern Spain were seeking God's presence together. What happened in the midst of this House of Prayer was that the level of hunger for God's presence began to increase. We all were discovering in a deeper dimension that His presence was needed to reach the city, that His presence needed to be pursued, and that we could not live without it.

Seek God fervently for His presence in your own life, in your own church, and in your city. This is what real life is all about. God loves to be sought after. His presence and Spirit will move us forward into realms of fruitfulness beyond our wildest imagination. But we must hoist our sails and catch the wind of His Spirit. The breath of His Spirit will change the face of everything, including our own lives. Larry Keefauver in his article, "His Presence: The key to Church Growth," says:

> The breath of God's Spirit must fill the church, empowering it to move forward into God's destiny. God's Spirit births every movement of the church. Without being Spirit or presence-driven, the church sits listlessly in time, like a sailboat going nowhere in a calm sea. We can use our paradigm as paddles and row as hard as we like, but the forward progress is negligible. Or, we can hoist our sails of worship, catch the wind of His Spirit and move forward into His purpose, plans and productivity in ministry.[2]

The question we must ask ourselves is, "Are we hungry enough to pursue God's presence?" The cost is high. In the House of Prayer in Spain we found that as we spent hour after hour in prayer, we were being stretched in our capacity to seek after God.

It will cost to seek God's presence. It will take diligence and time. We will have to clear our schedules of so much busyness if we want His presence. We will have to sacrifice, but it will be worth all the pain.

Are we willing to pay the price?

The Bible speaks about God's presence. God longs for us to build a house where He dwells. The following are verses to challenge you to pursue God's presence:

- **2 Chronicles 7:14.** *If My people, who are called by My name, will humble themselves and pray and seek My face and turn from their wicked ways, then will I hear from heaven and will forgive their sin and will heal their land.*

- **Isaiah 66:1-2a.** *This is what the LORD says: "Heaven is my throne, and the earth is my footstool. Where is the house that you will build for me? Where will my resting place be? Has not my hand made all these things, and so they came into being?" declares the LORD.*

- **Isaiah 56:7.** *"...these I will bring to my holy mountain and give them joy in my house of prayer. Their burnt offerings and sacrifices will be accepted on my altar; for my house will be called a house of prayer for all nations."*

- **2 Chronicles 7:15-16.** *Now my eyes will be open and my ears attentive to the prayers offered in this place. I have chosen and consecrated this temple so that my Name may be there forever. My eyes and my heart will always be there.*

- **Psalm 89:15-16.** *Blessed are those who have learned to acclaim you, who walk in the light of your presence, O LORD. They rejoice in your name all day long; they exalt in your righteousness.*

The testimony to what happens when God's presence arrives is quite astounding! Are we ready for it? Can we handle the depth of work His Spirit will do in our own individual lives that will prepare and empower us to reach this desperate and dying world? Here is a testimony of what actually happened when God showed up at the Azusa Street Revival in 1906:

> In that old building, with its low rafters and bare floors, God took strong men and women to pieces, and put them together again, for His glory. It was a tremendous overhauling process. Pride and self-assertion, self-importance and self-esteem, could not survive there. The religious ego preached its own funeral quickly.[3] Guido Kuwaws, "The Azusa Street Revival Part II"

When God's presence touches our prayer meetings and our lives, all flesh must die. We see the futility of our own ways of doing things, and we begin to see the majestic wisdom of God and the attractiveness of Jesus. We begin to line up with His ways, and what once was a barren way of trying to produce life becomes a supernatural encounter with the presence of the living God. This brings forth amazing fruit in every dimension of our lives. Pursuing God's presence is one of the keys to a deeper prayer life.

Doesn't this seem to be a better way of life than what many of us have tried for so many years?

> Shouldn't Jesus himself be the preeminent attraction? We can promote our church programs with precision and good marketing techniques, but when somebody who is blind or deaf gets healed, or a political leader gets saved, or once-barren land produces a bountiful harvest, people will flock to church. God is His own best promoter! He just shows up and effortlessly turns our routines into supernatural encounters that are life changing.[4] Rhonda Hughey, *Desperate for His Presence*

Hindrances to God's Presence

> Have you ever wondered if it is possible to get God's attention or attract His presence? And if it is possible, then why don't we spend more time doing those things that welcome His presence? God's Word establishes clear principles regarding His presence. There are things that prepare for and welcome the presence of the Lord—things like prayer, unity, worship, and a broken and contrite spirit. There are also things that cause Him to withdraw or remain at a distance.[5] Rhonda Hughey, *Desperate for His Presence*

In the rest of this chapter let's look at how to seek God's presence, not only personally, but also corporately as the Church. Jesus is knocking at the door of our cities.

Can you hear His knock?

Are you aware that your King wants to visit your city, but He will not force His way in when there is no invitation? It is the responsibility of the church to welcome His presence into the city. He is the honored guest. We must roll out the royal carpet for our King, and invite His glorious entrance into our city. We must do this together as the corporate church in the city.

The question we must ask ourselves is, "Can we live without Him in our city? Are we willing to unite and seek Him together as the city Church? Rhonda Hughey stresses the importance of God's blueprint of unity:

> It's not possible to have a lasting corporate impact on a city as a single congregation. God hasn't constructed the rules of life that way. It requires corporate unity and agreement to accomplish corporate results... God has ordained a corporate church in each city! There is something bigger than our local congregations! There should be one Shepherd and one King enthroned in our cities. We must start with a common vision and purpose and then build according to God's blueprint, not our own. We can't start with our own empire and then try to build up to who God is. He will step down to us in response to our desperate cry.[6]

We must seek for unity in our cities and contend for God's presence regardless of the cost. Look at the condition of your city. What is happening in the streets and neighborhoods around you? Watch the news and read the newspaper. Look at the people in your city. Let the condition of what you see break your heart.

What are the roadblocks to God's presence in your city and nation?

Just as there are roadblocks keeping you from reaching your destination when driving a car, there are roadblocks to God's entrance into your city. There are many obstacles to God's presence individually and corporately. The following are a few key barriers with verses relating to these obstacles. I encourage you to pray that God removes these roadblocks that keep His presence from entering your city. Pray that God removes them from your own heart.

- **Pride.** We are often self-righteous and think we are good, but Jesus is our example of humility. God hates pride, and He will not bring His manifest presence into our city when we are walking in pride. We often try to get to the highest position, but Jesus carried a towel and washed His disciple's feet.

In your relationships with one another, have the same mindset as Christ Jesus: Who, being in very nature God, did not consider equality with God something to be used to his own advantage rather, he made himself nothing by taking the very nature of a servant, being made in human likeness. And being found in appearance as a man, he humbled himself by becoming obedient to death—even death on a cross (Philippians 2:5-8).

- **Idolatry.** Idolatry diminishes God's glory. When the presence of God is not in a city, it is often because the Church is not seeking it. Whatever we substitute for our love for God becomes an idol. These idols may be sports, TV, material possessions, and many other attractions. Think about where you spend your time, and examine your own heart.

Who may ascend the mountain of the LORD? Who may stand in His holy place? The one who has clean hands and a pure heart, who does not trust in an idol, or swear by a false god (Psalm 24:3-4).

- **Immorality.** The temptations towards sexual sins are everywhere. Every believer must guard against this. Pray for purity in the body of Christ. God will make His presence known when His Church walks in holiness. Pray for purity in your own life.

Flee from sexual immorality. All other sins a person commits are outside his body, but whoever sins sexually, sins against their own body. Do you not know that your bodies are temples of the Holy Spirit, who is in you, whom you have received from God? You are not your own; you were bought at a price. Therefore honor God with your bodies (1 Corinthians 6:18-20).

- **Unbelief.** We must believe the promises of God and have faith that He will accomplish them in His timing. Unbelief denies his promises and power. He promises us that if we ask in His name, He will do it (John 14:13-14). Are you believing God's promises in your life?

And without faith it is impossible to please God, because anyone who comes to him must believe that he exists and that he rewards those who earnestly seek him (Hebrews 11:6).

- **Distractions.** Distractions are everywhere. We must give God unhurried time and undistracted hours. We can no longer get busy with secondary things when God wants our attention and desires that we seek one thing.

  One thing I ask of the LORD, this only do I seek: that I may dwell in the house of the LORD all the days of my life, to gaze on the beauty of the LORD and to seek him in his temple (Psalm 27:4).

- **Luke-warm hearts.** So many in the church have left their first love, and their hearts no longer are passionate towards God. They have settled for a luke-warm life. God wants us to be on fire for Him. One of the recurring prayers during the month-long prayer meeting in Spain was for the fire (fuego) of God!

  I know your deeds, that you are neither cold nor hot. I wish you were either one or the other! So, because you are lukewarm— neither hot nor cold—I am about to spit you out of my mouth (Revelation 3:15-16).

- **Religious spirit.** This is a counterfeit form of life and godliness. It may look good on the outside, but it is based on human wisdom and man-made agendas. It may have many programs, but it is a substitute for Jesus and is totally disconnected with real life.

  ... having a form of godliness but denying its power. Have nothing to do with them (2 Tim. 3:5).

- **Disunity.** God will not make His presence known to a disunified Church. We must learn to value the other parts of the body of Christ. We must see that we fit together and cannot reach the city by ourselves. We desperately need each other. Are you unified with other Christians? Do you have any broken relationships? See Psalm 133.

  I have given them the glory that you gave me, that they may be one as we are one—I in them and you in me—so that they may be brought to complete unity. Then the world will know that you sent me and have loved them even as you have loved me (John 17:22-23).

Let's pray this passionate prayer for God's presence by Tommy Tenney from his book called *The God Chasers:*

> *Father, we confess that we want to see change in our lives and in our church so we can bring about change in our city. Give us such a heart and passion after You that we may begin to see Your glory flow out of us to convict and save the lost. Release your presence through us as You did through Charles Finney when he walked through factories and saw workers drop to their knees under Your glory and cried out for forgiveness although not one word had been spoken or preached. May the faintest shadow of Your presence in our lives heal the sick and restore the lame we meet in the streets. Let your presence so saturate us that unsaved guests can't step into our homes or be around us with unrepentant hearts. May Your glory bring conviction in their lives that lead to salvation —not because of the words we say but because of Your presence and power in our heart.*

One thing that God wants us to realize is how very desperately He cares for the lost in our cities. He is a compassionate God, and the pain and cries in the city have touched His heart deeply. He wants us to partner with Him in bringing hope to our cities, but He cannot do this if there are barriers preventing His presence from entering the place where we live.

He is the answer to all the problems and pain. His presence in our cities will make all the difference. Let's partner with Him. Removing the barriers of his presence in our lives is one of the secrets to a deeper prayer life.

When we see the ruined condition of our cities and communities, it should break our hearts and stir us to prayer. We have underestimated the pain in God's heart over the devastation and brokenness of people who live in darkness. Isaiah 9:2 declares what the result would be when Jesus' presence came to earth: "The people walking in darkness have seen a great light" (NIV). God fully intends to continue to bring hope and restoration to forsaken, desolate communities, and He is looking for those who will partner with Him.[8] Rhonda Hughey, *Desperate for His Presence*

The Manifest Presence of God

When God's presence becomes a tangible reality in a community, the church then becomes a catalyst for growth. God's presence is more effective than our best church growth methods. When God's presence is tangible, supernatural ministry results and becomes a magnet for hungry souls and broken people."[9] Rhonda Hughey, *Desperate for His Presence*

There is a popular Christian song that we sang and prayed in Spain. The song goes like this, "Let it rain. Let it rain. Open the floodgates of heaven and let it rain!"

During the month the prayers were getting stronger, more intense, and they were uniting with more faith. There was a great desire for God to open the heavens and flood down His manifest presence upon the land. There was a heart-felt expectation that God had heard our prayers and would answer.

So we continued to pray that He would open the floodgates of heaven and come—raining His presence and fire on the land. Everyone was feeling the presence of God in the prayer room. The prayers continued non-stop throughout all of November. Lives were being changed radically. There was even a six-hour prayer meeting for healing with an invitation for all the sick to come for prayer. As God descends upon the land in southern Spain, His people are rising higher into the throne room of heaven. Rhonda exhorts us to come up higher and see from God's vantage point:

God longs to open doors of spiritual reality to us. He wants us to sit with Him in heavenly places. We must live with a spiritual vantage point from the throne room of God. The throne of God is the seat of His authority; it represents the place from which He rules and reigns over the nations. Jesus invites us to this place of authority and victory. We have to see the Lord! We have to accept the invitation to come up higher around the throne, to behold Jesus, to see Him and believe! Once you see this, you have hope; and once we see what God sees, then we can come into agreement with His purposes. If we cannot see God's kingdom purposes, we cannot agree with them![10]

What is the evidence of God's manifest presence upon a city and in your own life? Slowly meditate on these words as you think about God's presence in your city: renown, joy, praise, honor, awe, tremble, abundant prosperity, peace, boldness, miraculous signs and wonders, Holy Spirit, crown of splendor, royal diadem, holy, great delight, and married. What does God's manifest presence look like, and how do things begin to change?

- **A new spiritual identity.** God's people begin to be personally transformed. They begin to know their spiritual identity in Christ. There is an increased intimacy with the Lord, both corporately and individually. The Christians in the city begin to release God's glory to others. They bring light into the darkness and carry His presence wherever they go. In what way do you carry God's presence—His peace, joy, kindness, etc.—with you wherever you go?

  Then this city will bring me renown, joy, praise and honor before all nations on earth that hear of all the good things I do for it; and they will be in awe and will tremble at the abundant prosperity and peace I provide for it (Jeremiah 33:9).

- **A new spiritual authority.** A personal and corporate refining takes place. There is no more compromise or complacency, but there is steady growth in holiness. Passion for Jesus becomes the highest priority, and the Church has a new spiritual authority that greatly impacts the city. The Spirit of God is released through the Church radically, and signs and wonders take place. How is God's authority increasing in your life?

  Now, Lord, consider their threats and enable your servants to speak your word with great boldness. Stretch out your hand to heal and perform signs and wonders through the name of your holy servant Jesus (Acts 4:29-31).

- **A new spiritual purpose.** The Church begins to really know her purpose, and begins to love and serve the city. Captives are healed and set free through the Spirit of God. Strongholds are broken. The Church is an agent of change in the city. People are drawn to Jesus and the Church because God's people are carrying God's presence and glory into the community. Think about your spiritual purpose and God's power. Are people drawn to you because they are attracted to God's Spirit in your life?

  So he said to me, "This is the word of the LORD to Zerubbabel: 'Not by might nor by power, but by my Spirit,' says the LORD Almighty (Zech. 4:6).

- **A transformation takes place.** City transformation and fruitfulness begins to take place. The Kingdom of God begins to touch the earth, and kingdom vision is released. There is city transformation that reflects God's glory and beauty. The city has a new name and is no longer deserted or desolate. Are you experiencing God's delight and an increasing fruitfulness and life transformation in your life?

  You will be a crown of splendor in the LORD's hand, a royal diadem in the hand of your God. No longer will they call you Deserted, or name your land Desolate. But you will be called Hephzibah, and your land Beulah; for the LORD will take great delight in you, and your land will be married (Isaiah 62:3-4).

The glory of God is contagious. Hunger for His presence increases. Many individuals who had been praying with us in Spain say that their lives had been changed even after only a few days. All of a sudden everyone saw what was really important in life.

I heard passionate prayers. I saw many tears. I heard many cries for God's presence to come to the city. God is doing something big. Everything was narrowing down to one thing—seeking God and His manifest presence in that area of the world.

We invite you to seek the Lord for your city. Give God extravagant time. It is time for us to hunger for His presence. We can't do anything without the presence of Jesus.

We've come to the end of this book. We've look at developing a deeper relationship with God in prayer from many different dimensions. We've learned many secrets to a deeper prayer life. In this last chapter we've seen how seeking God and going *deeper still* leads to God's presence in our cities.

As we look at the world situation, we realize that the hour is extremely urgent, and it's time to go deeper with God both individually and corporately as the Church. It's time to contend for God's presence in prayer. Will you join me in this great endeavor to go *deeper still* with God for such a time as this? It will be the best thing that we can do. He longs for our intimacy.

> Information doesn't transform cities. Conferences can't transform a city! Education can't transform a city! Having citywide ministry programs or large networks cannot transform a city. Only the presence of Jesus can bring transformation, and only individual people willing to get on the altars of prayer to contend for His presence will become the kindling for God's fire.[11]
> Rhonda Hughey, *Desperate for His Presence*

Deeper Still Life Application
How to Cultivate God's Presence

In this final chapter, we looked at pursuing God's presence, hindrances, and the manifest presence of God. Carefully meditate on this chapter before answering the following questions. This exercise is to help you consider whether there are any hindrances to God's presence in your life. Write down your answers.

- How hungry am I for God's presence? - Study the following Scriptures: Isaiah 56:7; 66:1; 2 Chronicles 7:14-16; and Psalm 89:15.
- Is there any pride in my life? - Meditate on Philippians 1:5-8. Write down any areas of pride.
- Are there any idols in my life? - List them. For example: TV, sports, materialism, and so on. Study Psalm 24:3-4.
- Is there any unbelief in my life? - If so, in what areas? See Hebrews 11:6.
- What is distracting me from seeking God wholeheartedly? - Meditate on Psalm 27:4.
- Is there any area where Satan is tempting me sexually? - Am I living a sexually pure life? Study 1 Corinthians 6:18-20.
- Am I united with others? - Do I value others in the body of Christ who are different than me? How am I cultivating unity? See John 17:22-23.
- Am I praying for God's presence in my city? - In what way am I involved in contending for His presence in my city? See Jeremiah 33:9.

Write a prayer to the Lord, bringing the answers to your questions before His throne in prayer.

How to Help Others
Cultivate God's Presence

Get together with a group or individual and carefully study this chapter. Give each person time to personally answer the above questions on a sheet of paper. You may want to have each one do this beforehand so they can have plenty of time to think through each answer. Then get together in a group and share your answers. Give each one enough time to fully express themselves. Carefully study the verses along with the questions. Then have a time of prayer together, repenting of any roadblocks that hinders God's presence. End your prayer time by praying "My Prayer to God."

My Prayer to God

Father, I pray that You will visit us, and make Your presence known in my life and in my city. Give me faith to believe that You can change my city. Let Your Kingdom come on earth as it is in heaven. Help me to cultivate Your presence in my life. I choose to partner with You for transformation in my city. I choose to walk in humility. Help me to contend for my city in prayer. Remove the distractions and any barriers in my life that keep me from Your presence. [Repent of any barriers in your life.] I repent of any pride or personal idols. [Name them.] Take away any luke-warmness in my heart, and set me on fire for You. I thank You for the new spiritual identity You will bring into my city as I pray. You say in Jeremiah 33:9: "Then this city will bring me renown, joy, praise and honor before all nations on earth that hear of all the good things I do for it; and they will be in awe and will tremble at the abundant prosperity and peace I provide for it."

I want to worship only You. Help me to walk in holiness and purity. Take me deeper still in my prayer life, and help me to practice all of the secrets to a deeper prayer life that I have learned in this book. I want to know You. "Blessed are those who have learned to acclaim you, who walk in the light of your presence, O Lord" (Psalm 89:15). "You make known to me the path of life; you will fill me with joy in your presence, with eternal pleasures at your right hand" (Psalm 16:11). "One thing I ask of the LORD, this is what I seek: that I may dwell in the house of the LORD all the days of my life, to gaze upon the beauty of the LORD and to seek him in his temple... Hear my voice when I call, O LORD... My heart says of you, "Seek his face!" Your face, LORD, I will seek" (Psalm 27:4, 7a, 8). In Jesus' name, amen.

Deeper Still
Secrets to a Deeper Prayer Life

Conclusion

Deep calls to deep in the roar of your waterfalls;
all your waves and breakers have swept over me.
By day the Lord directs his love,
at night his song is with me—
a prayer to the God of my life.
Psalm 42:7-8

Deep calls unto Deep. God is calling you to go *deeper still* in prayer and in your personal relationship with Him. As you move forth in your life journey, take what you have learned in this book seriously—carefully hiding these secrets in your heart on a daily basis. Go over them again and again. They are designed to empower you in a moment of time when you need a specific secret to help you in your personal prayer life.

This book, *Deeper Still: Secrets to a Deeper Prayer Life* ends, but I pray that your life in prayer and intercession expands deeper, wider, and higher than ever before. Let the practice of prayer and the hunger for intimacy be the highest ambition of your life. May you go *deeper still* in knowing God with an ever-increasing joy in His presence.

- May God richly bless you as you go deeper in your relationship with the Father, the Son, and the Holy Spirit.

- May you be one who prays with strategy and insight initiated from heaven's throne.

- May you learn to embrace the rich treasures discovered in the dark nights when God seems hidden from your view.

- May your prayers be powerful and effective even in the most impossible situations you face in life.

- May you learn the secret beauty of prayer and fasting and be one who pursues God's manifest presence for your personal life, your city, and your nation.

As you go *deeper still*, may God strengthen your inner being and establish you with deeper roots in the soil of His abundant love. I pray that you may be filled to the fullness of God, as you grasp how wide and how long and high and deep the love of Christ is. Always remember that His love will direct you by day, and His song will be with you at night.

I close with this prayer for you from Ephesians 3:16-19:

I pray that out of his glorious riches he may strengthen you
with power through his Spirit in your inner being,
so that Christ may dwell in your hearts through faith.
And I pray that you, being rooted and established in love,
may have power together with all the saints,
to grasp how wide and long and high and deep
is the love of Christ, and to know
this love that surpasses knowledge—
that you may be filled to the measure
of all the fullness of God.

About the Author

Debbie Przybylski is the founder and director of Intercessors Arise International, a part of the ministry of Elijah Company, Inc. The vision of Intercessors Arise International is to ignite the fire of prayer and worship worldwide and see a multitude of intercessors from every nation released in strategic prayer for the furtherance of the gospel.

Debbie's passion is to see intercessors at work stirring the nations and setting captives free throughout the world by the ministry of prayer. She believes intercessors must be trained, encouraged, and released for the end-times harvest. Debbie's husband, Norman, is the founder and director of Elijah Company, Inc. Debbie serves alongside him in their ministry of training, equipping, and mentoring future and presently active cross-cultural workers by identifying, instructing, imparting, and impelling them to God's designated field of service.

Some related aspects of training offered by the Przybylskis are seminars and training courses in intercession, Houses of Prayer, missions, evangelism, breaking free from spiritual strongholds, and the Lighthouse of Prayer ministry. Norm and Debbie have ministered in over 65 nations. They envision intercession and missions uniting for global harvest.

Norm and Debbie live in Grandview, Missouri. Debbie is on staff with the International House of Prayer Missions Base (IHOPKC) in Kansas City.

Books by Debbie Przybylski

Intercessors Arise: Personal Prayer that Changes the World. Colorado Springs, CO: NavPress, 2008.

Breakthrough Prayer: Praying God's Truth, Destroying Enemy Lies. Charleston, SC: CreateSpace, 2013.

Ascending the Heights in Prayer: Touching Heaven, Changing Earth. Charleston, SC: CreateSpace, 2013.

Deeper Still: Secrets to a Deeper Prayer Life. Charleston, SC: CreateSpace, 2013.

24/7 Prayer Arise: Building the House of Prayer in Your City. Charleston, SC: CreateSpace, 2013.

Intercessors Arise International

Arise, shine, for your light has come,
and the glory of the Lord rises upon you.
Isaiah 60:1

The vision of Intercessors Arise International is to ignite the fire of prayer worldwide and see a multitude of intercessors from every nation released in strategic prayer and worship for the furtherance of the gospel. We desire to encourage the strength and vision of intercession worldwide to see a release of God's power and glory. We envision Houses of Prayer established in every city in every nation.

Our Mission Statement

Igniting the Fire of Prayer Worldwide

A Multitude of United Intercessors and Worshippers Released
in Strategic Prayer for the Furtherance of the Gospel Worldwide -
A House of Prayer in Every City in Every Nation

The corporate strength and power of united intercession and worship will allow the spiritual breakthrough needed to release the power of God in every nation.

May we passionately seek God for breakthroughs.
A mighty harvest is at our doorstep.
May intercessors arise for such a time as this!

For further information, see *www.intercessorsrise.org.*

Services Offered

Intercessors Arise International
Elijah Company, Inc.

Conferences, Seminars, and Training Retreats

Norm and Debbie Przybylski travel worldwide teaching, training, and mentoring together on various themes related to missions and intercession. Topics include prayer, intercession, 24/7 prayer, breaking strongholds, power evangelism, world missions, and missionary training. One of their specialties is their Missionary Training Camps that are known to launch people into their missionary call. For information about hosting an event with Norm and Debbie in your church or city, email them at contact@elijahcompany.org. You can visit both of their websites at: www.elijahcompany.org and www.intercessorsarise.org.

Books, CDs, and other Resources

The Przybylskis have produced resources relating to subjects they teach. They have produced several articles and materials relating to prayer and missions. Norm and Debbie have also produced an Ekballo Elijah Company Training Manual and a set of CDs of their Elijah Company Equipping Seminar. Debbie has written several books and articles on prayer. You will find out more about their training materials on their websites.

Intercessors Arise International Website

Intercessors Arise International has a vision to unite, motivate, train, and network the corporate strength and vision of intercessors worldwide to see a release of God's power and glory for the furtherance of world evangelization. The Intercessors Arise International website is designed for intercessors for this purpose. In this website there are many training and teaching materials related to prayer and intercession. For further information, see www.intercessorsarise.org.

The Elijah Company Website

The Elijah Company website is designed to empower God's people in their calling to reach the nations. This website along with Elijah Company training is designed to equip, inform, train, and mentor God's people by identifying, instructing, imparting, and impelling them to God's designated place of service. See www.elijahcompany.org, for further information.

International School of Prayer

The Intercessors Arise International website includes an International School of Prayer designed for training in intercession and prayer for intercessors in every nation. Included are articles covering a wide variety of topics for those interested in developing their prayer life. This school includes training for beginners as well as seasoned intercessors. The International School of Prayer is informative, Biblical, and motivational. If you would like to become a part of this prayer school, see www.intercessorsarise.org. This is still in the developmental stage.

The Intercessors Arise International Network

The Intercessors Arise International Network is designed to ignite the fire of prayer worldwide and is a companion site to Intercessors Arise International. It is interactive, informative, and motivational. In this network a member can connect with others worldwide who are involved in prayer. You will be able to unite with those who are starting 24/7 Houses of Prayer in their city. Discover what God is doing around the world in prayer today and how you can be a part of it. To join this global network, see www.intercessorsarise.ning.com.

Training through the Internet

Norm and Debbie provide teaching and encouragement on prayer or missions through their email training. These email networks are free! Join hundreds worldwide who receive these training emails described below:

- **Intercessors Arise International** is an email publication sent worldwide for intercessors and those interested in growing in prayer and intercession. It is designed to train, encourage, motivate, inform, and release individuals and prayer groups in intercession. If you would like to subscribe to this free publication, see www.intercessorsarise.org.

- **Intercessors Arise America** is an email publication for intercessors in America. It is similar to the above except occasionally it may have added information regarding issues in America. If you would like to subscribe to this free publication, see www.intercessorsarise.org.

- **Intercesores Arriba** is an email publication for Spanish-speaking intercessors interested in growing in prayer and intercession. It is designed to train, motivate, and release individuals and prayer groups in intercession throughout the Spanish-speaking world. If you would like to subscribe to this free publication, see www.intercessorsarise.org.

For further information regarding Elijah Company, Inc. and Intercessors Arise International, contact:

Elijah Company, Inc.
P.O. Box 396
Grandview, MO 64030
Email: contact@elijahcompany.org.
Websites: www.intercessorsarise.org, www.elijahcompany.org.

Recommended Reading

Bickle, Mike. *Passion for Jesus*. Orlando, FL: Creation House, 1993.

Bickle, Mike and Dana Chandler. *The Rewards of Fasting: Experiencing the Power and Affections of God*. Kansas City, MO: Forerunner Books, 2005.

Blackaby, Henry and Richard. *Experiencing God Day by Day*. Nashville, TN: B&H Publishing Group, 2003.

Bounds, E. M. *E. M. Bounds on Prayer*. New Kensington, PA: Whitaker House, 1997.

Campbell, Wesley and Stacey. *Praying the Bible: The Book of Prayers*. Ventura, CA: Regal Books, 2002.

Campbell, Wesley and Stacey. *Praying the Bible: The Pathway to Spirituality*. Ventura, CA: Gospel Light, 2003.

Cooke, Graham. *Drawing Close*. Grand Rapids, MI: Chosen Books, 2005.

Damazio, Frank. *Seasons of Intercession*. Portland, OR: BT Publishing, 1998.

Dawson, John. *Taking Our Cities for God*. Lake Mary, FL: Creation House, 1990.

Dawson, Joy. *Intercession: Thrilling and Fulfilling*. Seattle, WA: YWAM Publishing, 1997.

Foster, Richard. *Prayer: Finding the Heart's True Home*. London: Hodder & Stoughton, 1992.

Goll, Jim. *The Lost Art of Intercession*. Shippensburg, PA: Destiny Image Publishers, Inc., 1997.

Goll, Jim. *Kneeling on the Promises*. Grand Rapids, MI: Chosen Books, 2006.

Greig, Peter and Roberts, Dave. *Red Moon Rising*. Eastbourne, England:

Relevant Books, associated with Kingsway Publishers, 2003.

Grubb, Norman. *Rees Howells, Intercessor.* Fort Washington, PA: Christian Literature Crusade, 1962.

Haan, Dr. Cornell. *The Lighthouse Movement Handbook.* Sisters, OR: Multnomah Publishers, 1999.

Hawthorne, Steve and Kendrick, Graham. *Prayerwalking.* Orlando, FL: Creation House, 1993.

Howard, Michael. *Tales of an African Intercessor.* Kansas City, MO: Out of Africa Publishers, 1998.

Hughey, Rhonda. *Desperate for His Presence.* Minneapolis, MN: Bethany House, 2004.

Jacobs, Cindy. *Possessing the Gates of the Enemy: A Manual for Militant Intercession.* Grand Rapids, MI: Chosen Books, 1991.

Johnstone, Patrick. *Operation World.* Waynesboro, GA: Paternoster Publishing, 2001.

Meyer, Joyce. *Battlefield of the Mind.* Tulsa, OK: Harrison House, 1995.

Murray, Andrew. *Andrew Murray on Prayer.* New Kensington, PA: Whitaker House, 1998.

Omartian, Stormie. *The Power of a Praying Woman.* Eugene, OR: Harvest House Publishers, 2002.

Pierce, Chuck with Dickson, John. *The Worship Warrior.* Ventura, CA: Regal Books, 2002.

Pray! Magazine. Colorado Springs, CO: The Navigators, 2007.

Prince, Derek. *Shaping History through Prayer and Fasting.* New Kensington, PA: Whitaker House, 1973.

Przybylski, Debbie. *Intercessors Arise: Personal Prayer that Changes the World.* Colorado Springs, CO: NavPress, 2008.

Przybylski, Debbie. *24/7 Prayer Arise: Building the House of Prayer in Your City.* Charleston, SC: CreateSpace, 2013.

Sandford, John Loren. *Healing the Nations: A Call to Global Intercession.* Grand Rapids, MI: Chosen Books, 2000.

Sheets, Dutch. *Intercessory Prayer.* Ventura, CA: Regal Books, 1996.

Silvoso, Ed. *That None Should Perish.* Ventura: CA: Regal Books, 1994.

Smith, Alice. *Beyond the Veil.* Ventura, CA: Regal Books, 1997.

Smith, Eddie and Alice. *Drawing Closer to God's Heart.* Lake Mary, FL: Charisma House, 2002.

Smith, Eddie and Alice. *Spiritual Housecleaning.* Ventura, CA: Regal Books, 2003.

Sorge, Bob. *Secrets of the Secret Place.* Kansas City, MO: Oasis House, 2006.

Sorge, Bob. *The Fire of Delayed Answers.* Canandaigua, NY: Oasis House, 1999.

Tozer, A. W. *The Knowledge of the Holy.* San Francisco, CA: Harper & Row Publishers, 1961.

Towns, Elmer L. *Fasting for Spiritual Breakthrough.* Ventura, CA: Regal Books, 1996.

Wagner, Peter. *Prayer Shield,* Ventura, CA: Regal Books, 1992.

Wilkinson, Bruce. *The Prayer of Jabez.* Sisters, OR: Multnomah Publishers, 2000.

For a more extended reading list, see www.intercessorsarise.org.

Endnotes

Chapter One
Deeper in Knowing God

[1] Dr. William Moses Tidwell, *Effective Illustrations.*

[2] Henry and Richard Blackaby, *Experiencing God Day-by-Day* (Makati City: Church Strengthening Ministry, 1998), 2.

[3] Eugenia Price, *Share My Pleasant Stones* (Grand Rapid, MI: Zondervan Publishing House, 1957).

[4] Henry and Richard Blackaby, *Experiencing God Day-by-Day* (Makati City: Church Strengthening Ministry, 1998), 217.

[5] E. M. Bounds, *The Possibilities of Prayer* as found in *E. M. Bounds on Prayer* (New Kensington: PA: Whitaker House, 1997), 275.

[6] E. M. Bounds, pg. 283.

[7] Noah Webster, *Webster's Dictionary* (San Francisco, CA: Foundation for American Christian Education, 1985).

[8] E. M. Bounds, *The Possibilities of Prayer* as found in *E. M. Bounds on Prayer* (New Kensington: PA: Whitaker House, 1997), 273.

[9] Newscaster Paul Harvey, written by John Nelson Darby.

[10] E. M. Bounds, *The Possibilities of Prayer* as found in *E. M. Bounds on Prayer* (New Kensington: PA: Whitaker House, 1997), 282.

Chapter Two
Deeper in Glorifying Christ

[1] Francis Frangipane, *Holiness, Truth and the Presence of God* (Cedar Rapids, IA: Arrow Publications, 1986), 34.

[2] Richard J. Mouw, *Uncommon Decency* (Downers Grove, IL: InterVarsity Press, 1992), 149-150.

[3] Andrew Murray, *Abide in Christ* as found in *Andrew Murray on Prayer* (New Kensington, PA: Whitaker House, 1998), 141.

[4] E. M. Bounds, *The Possibilities of Prayer* as found in *E. M. Bounds on Prayer* (New Kensington, PA: Whitaker House, 1997), 227.

[5] Andrew Murray, *The Secret of Intercession* as found in *Andrew Murray on Prayer* (New Kensington, PA: Whitaker House, 1998), 606.

[6] Andrew Murray, pg. 533.

[7] Andrew Murray, pg. 533.

[8] Andrew Murray, *God's Best Secrets: Daily Devotional Meditations* (Grand Rapids, MI: Zondervan Publishing House, 1979), January 31.

[9] Noah Webster, *Webster's Dictionary* (San Francisco, CA: Foundation for American Christian Education, 1985).

[10] Phillip Schaff.

Chapter Three
Deeper in Partnering with The Holy Spirit

[1] Andrew Murray, *With Christ in the School of Prayer* as found in *Andrew Murray on Prayer* (New Kensington, PA: Whitaker House, 1998), 427.

[2] Dutch Sheets, *Watchman Prayer* (Ventura, CA: Regal Books, 2000), 151.

[3] Andrew Murray, *With Christ in the School of Prayer* as found in *Andrew Murray on Prayer* (New Kensington, PA: Whitaker House, 1998), 427-428.

[4] Samuel Shoemaker.

[5] James Graf, "No Longer Normal" (Colorado Springs, CO: The Navigators, Pray! magazine, Issue 36, May/June, 2003), 36.

[6] James Graf, pg. 35.

[7] James Graf, pg. 36.

[8] R. A. Torrey, "How to Promote and Conduct a Successful Revival".

[9] Mel Winger, "Supernatural Prayer Partners" (Colorado Springs, CO: The Navigators, Pray! magazine, Issue 36, May/June, 2003), 31.

[10] Terry Gooding, (Colorado Springs, CO: The Navigators, Pray! magazine, Issue 50, September-October, 2005), 20.

[11] Dick Eastman, (Colorado Springs, CO: The Navigators, Pray! magazine, Issue 50, September-October, 2005), 19-20.

[12] Norman Przybylski, Elijah Company, Inc.

[13] Dick Eastman, (Colorado Springs, CO: The Navigators, Pray! magazine, Issue 50, September-October, 2005), 23.

Chapter Four
Deeper in Strategic Prayer

[1] Michael Howard, *Proven Arrows of Intercession* (Kansas City, MO: Out of Africa Publishers, 1999), 87-88.

[2] Michael Howard, pg. 84.

[3] Michael Howard, pg. 87.

[4] Michael Howard, pgs. 30-31.

[5] E. M. Bounds, *The Possibilities of Prayer* as found in *E. M. Bounds on*

Prayer (New Kensington, PA: Whitaker House, 1997), 214.

[6] Andrew Murray, compiled by Al Bryant, *Daily Secrets of Christian Living: A Daily Devotional, Unceasing Devotion* (Uhrichsville, OH: Barbour Publishing, Inc., 2008), January 23.

[7] Dorthy Haskins, *A Practical Guide to Prayer,* 1951.

[8] E. M. Bounds, *Power Through Prayer* as found in *E. M. Bounds on Prayer* (New Kensington, PA: Whitaker House, 1997), 486.

[9] E. M. Bounds, pg. 484-485.

[10] Graham Cooke, *Drawing Close* (Grand Rapids, MI: Chosen Books, 2005), 62-63.

[11] Graham Cooke, pg. 70.

[12] Henry and Richard Blackaby, *Experiencing God Day-by-Day* (Makati City: Church Strengthening Ministry, 1998), 124.

Chapter Five
Deeper in Spiritual Insight

[1] Jim Goll, *Father Forgive Us!* (Shippensburg, PA: Destiny Image Publishers, 2000), 189.

[2] Jim Goll, 189-190.

[3] Noah Webster, *Webster's Dictionary* (San Francisco, CA: Foundation for American Christian Education, 1985).

[4] Jim Goll, *Father Forgive Us!* (Shippensburg, PA: Destiny Image Publishers, 2000), 191.

[5] Dick Eastman, "Prayer Siege" (Colorado Springs, CO: The Navigators, Pray! magazine, Issue 36, May-June, 2003), 41.

[6] Dick Eastman, pg. 40.

[7] Eddie and Alice Smith, *Drawing Closer to God's Heart* (Lake Mary, FL: Charisma House, 2001), 192.

[8] Dick Eastman, *"Prayer Siege"* (Colorado Springs, CO: The Navigators, Pray! magazine, Issue 36, May-June, 2003), 40.

[9] Graham Cooke, *Crafted Prayer* (Grand Rapids, MI: Chosen Books, 2004), 69.

[10] Graham Cooke, pg. 70.

[11] Graham Cooke, pg. 40.

Chapter Six
Deeper in Disciplining the Soul

[1] Tracey McCary Rhodes, "Clinging to God in the Darkness" (Colorado

Springs, CO: The Navigators, Pray! magazine, Issue 46, January-February, 2005), 34.

[2] Lori Wilke, *Requirements for Greatness* (Shippensburgh, PA: Destiny Im age Publishers, Inc., 1996), 139.

[3] Lori Wilke, Pg. 142.

[4] Tracey McCary Rhodes, "Clinging to God in the Darkness" (Colorado Springs, CO: The Navigators, Pray! magazine, Issue 46, January-February, 2005), 37.

[5] Michael Card, (Colorado Springs, CO: The Navigators, Pray! magazine, Issue 46, March-April, 2005), 36.

[6] Graham Cooke, *Drawing Close* (Grand Rapids, MI: Chosen Books, 2005), 74-75.

[7] *Today in the Word,* July, 1989, pg. 27.

[8] Michael Card, (Colorado Springs, CO: The Navigators, Pray! Issue 46, March-April, 2005), 35.

[9] Graham Cooke, *Drawing Close* (Grand Rapids, MI: Chosen Books, 2005), 77.

[10] Graham Cooke, *When the Lights Go Out* (Grand Rapids, MI: Chosen Books, 2005), 39.

[11] Graham Cooke, pg. 15.

[12] Noah Webster, *Webster's Dictionary* (San Francisco, CA: Foundation for American Christian Education, 1985).

[13] Graham Cooke, *When the Lights Go Out* (Grand Rapids, MI: Chosen Books, 2005), 55-56.

Chapter Seven
Deeper in Effective Prayer

[1] Smith Wigglesworth, 65.

2. E.M. Bounds, *The Possibilities of Prayer* as found in *E. M. Bounds on Prayer* (New Kensington, PA: Whitaker House, 1997), 211.

[3] E.M. Bounds, *The Necessity of Prayer* as found in *E. M. Bounds on Prayer* (New Kensington, PA: Whitaker House, 1997), 136.

[4] Noah Webster, *Webster's Dictionary* (San Francisco, CA: Foundation for American Christian Education, 1985).

[5] E.M. Bounds, *The Necessity of Prayer* as found in *E. M. Bounds on Prayer* (New Kensington, PA: Whitaker House, 1997), 134.

[6] A. W. Tozer, *The Christian Handbook.*

[7] Janet Leighton.

[8] Evelyn Christianson.

[9] A. W. Tozer.

Chapter Eight
Deeper in a Life of Fasting

[1] Dr. Kingsley A. Fletcher, *Prayer and Fasting* (New Kensington, PA: Whitaker House, 1992).

[2] Bill Bright, *The Transforming Power of Prayer and Fasting* (Orlando, FL: New Life Publications, 1997), 22.

[3] Alice Smith, *Beyond the Veil* (Ventura, CA: Regal Books, 1997), 177.

[4] Eddie and Alice Smith, *Drawing Closer to God's Heart* (Lake Mary, FL: Charisma House, 2001), 156.

[5] Eddie and Alice Smith, pg. 158.

[6] James Packer, *Your Father Loves You* (Colorado Springs, CO: Harold Shaw Publishers, 1986), 14.

[7] Elmer Towns, *Fasting for Spiritual Breakthrough* (Ventura, CA: Regal Books, 1996).

[8] Frank Damazio, *Seasons of Intercession* (Portland, OR: BT Publishing, 1998), 161.

[9] Andrew Murray, *With Christ in the School of Prayer* (Old Tappen, NJ: Fleming H. Revell Company, 1979), 74.

[10] Charles Finney.

[11] Frank Damazio, *Seasons of Intercession* (Portland, OR: BT Publishing, 1998), 166.

Chapter Nine
Deeper in Passionate Fervency

[1] Bill Gothard, *The Power of Crying Out* (Sisters: OR: Multnomah Publishers, Inc., 2002), 13.

[2] Bill Gothard, pg. 19.

[3] Bill Gothard, pg. 37.

[4] Rick Joyner, "Lessons on the Welsh Revival" (Wilksboro, NC: The Morningstar Journal, MorningStar Publications, Inc.), 66.

[5] Rick Joyner, pg. 67.

[6] Noah Webster, *Webster's Dictionary* (San Francisco, CA: Foundation for American Christian Education, 1985).

[7] Winkie Pratney, "The Nature of Revival" (Wilksboro, NC: The Morningstar Journal, MorningStar Publications, Inc.), 20.

[8] Rick Joyner, "Lessons on the Welsh Revival" (Wilksboro, NC: The Morningstar Journal, MorningStar Publications, Inc.), 67.

[9] Rick Joyner, "The Welsh Revival" (Wilksboro, NC: The Morningstar Journal,

MorningStar Publications, Inc.), 40.

[10] Our Daily Bread, April 24.

[11] Andrew Murray, *The Ministry of Intercession* as found in *Andrew Murray on Prayer* (New Kensington, PA: Whitaker House, 1998), 556.

[12] Rhonda Hughey, *Desperate for His Presence* (Minneapolis, MN: Bethany House, 2004), 199.

[13] Rhonda Hughey, pg. 202.

[14] George Otis, Jr., unpublished teaching notes.

[15] Rhonda Hughey, *Desperate for His Presence* (Minneapolis, MN: Bethany House, 2004), 199-200.

Chapter Ten
Deeper in God's Presence

[1] Rhonda Hughey, *Desperate for His Presence* (Minneapolis, MN: Bethany House, 2004), 34.

[2] Larry Keefauver, "His Presence: The Key to Church Growth" (Ministries Today, September-October, 2002), 51-52.

[3] Guido Kuwaws, "The Azusa Street Revival Part II" (Global Revival News, www.sendrevival.com).

[4] Rhonda Hughey, *Desperate for His Presence* (Minneapolis, MN: Bethany House, 2004), 35.

[5] Rhonda Hughey, pg. 68.

[6] Ronda Hughey, pg. 73-74.

[7] Tommy Tenney, *The God Chasers* (Shippensburg, PA: Destiny Image Publishers, Inc ., 2001), 117.

[8] Rhonda Hughey, *Desperate for His Presence* (Minneapolis, MN: Bethany House, 2004), 66.

[9] Rhonda Hughey, pg. 34.

[10] Rhonda Hughey, pg. 161-162.

[11] Rhonda Hughey, pg. 195.